MERVIN L. EVANS

Author: The Case for Black America

A New Direction 2014

Community People Press

Lynette A. Bigelow

Publisher

978-148139127   **Copyright 2013**

X

Mervin L Evans

PORPONENT

CALIFORNIA EVANS CHILD PROTECTION ACT

Ballot Measure

Requires 1-Strike 50 Year Prison Term for Crimes Against Kids

Requires 1-Strike 25 Year Prison Term for Adult Rape

Measure creates 25 Cent Beer - Wine Tax for

Better Law Enforcement to Protect Kids

There is No Public Policy that can allow 12,000 Adult Women

Rapes and 350,000 Kids to be Abused in the State of California,

Every Year!

WHY SAVE OUR CITIES

Cities and their surrounding inner-ring suburbs--what we will here call "metro" or "urban" regions--are the neglected stepchildren of American politics. More than half the population lives in them,1 and they suffer from all sorts of problems--from ghetto crime, unemployment, and racial segregation to environmentally-degrading and fiscally unbalanced suburban sprawl--but they are not subjects of constructive political debate. Commonly, indeed, discussion of our urban areas serves only as an occasion to express despair about economic dysfunction and social disintegration, and the resistance of both to political remedy.

That despair is justified, we are just as commonly told, by an Iron Law of Urban Decay: As incomes rise, workers move to suburbia; when suburbs mature, they resist paying taxes to support the metro core; as the tax base declines and services deteriorate, the middle-class flees, leading to further erosion; poverty concentrates among those left behind, and they become "different" disconnected from labor markets, without role models for advancement, lacking the human or financial capital even for bootstrap-pulling. In this context, we are told, the best that can be hoped from central cities is peace, or at least a segregation of the violence.

The best that can be hoped   for suburbia is . . . well, more suburbia. But further sprawl   only erodes the tax base of inner-ring suburbs, wedging their   residents between the spreading deterioration of the urban core   and the new roads, sewers, and schools for their increasingly   distant suburban "neighbors" on the edge. For their problems, angered inner-ring suburbanites tend to blame their more proximate neighbors in the central cities, people generally poorer and darker than themselves. Meanwhile, the wealthy   seek to insulate themselves--taking refuge in luxury urban   high-rises, or cloistered condo communities, or exclusionist   "favored quarters" of exurban development.

It is an ugly business, all the more so because it does not have   to be this way. If we wanted, we could reconstruct our   metropolitan regions. Taking full advantage of their dense   concentrations of people, skill, and infrastructure, we could   transform them from sites of hideous squalor, stark inequality,   and numbing natural destruction to vibrant centers of highwage, environmentally-sustainable economic activity and civil   social life. If we did, the benefits would be massive. Most   directly, metro reconstruction would markedly improve the   welfare of urban populations. More broadly, it would make substantial inroads on addressing the ruinous inequality and   declining living standards that currently define national   economic life. Finally, with the economy conditioning most of   the rest of our lives together, such reconstruction would have   large political and social benefits. We would regain some   measure of democracy and social peace among the people of   this country, making meaningful our now-fragile   commitments to shared citizenship, by focusing resources where most people actually live.

Despite these benefits, any serious project of reconstruction   will need to be fought for. That fight will require a wideranging alliance of interests: large numbers of people, now   divided from one another, must be persuaded of their common   stake in its success. And persuasion depends on the availability   of a plausible project capable of uniting these different   interests. Can such a project be stated? We think so, and   present a case for our affirmative answer here.

For reasons of space, we present the project schematically, without reference to the particular settings and histories--in cities as diverse as Milwaukee, Minneapolis-St. Paul, Portland, Seattle, and Cleveland--that inspire our confidence   in the possibilities of metro reconstruction. Furthermore,   while we have included lots of details about what needs to be   done and by whom, we understand that such details are   provisional: the best way to proceed will undoubtedly differ   from case to case, and, as projects of this kind unfold, we will   all learn more about the relative advantages of alternative   strategies. Still, enough is known now about what works, and   what does not, that a new urban agenda can be stated. And the   stakes are high enough to think, we believe not irrationally,   that urban politics and policy might once again be rescued   from obscurity and despair, and made an issue for political debate and popular mobilization.

Before getting to that agenda and its politics, however, we need first to make the case that something is worth doing, and   that it can in fact be done--that the Iron Law of Urban Decay is   imposed by political artifice, not nature.

Why Save Cities?

How did cities get into their current mess? There is no simple answer, but an important piece of the puzzle lies in American public policy. That policy is, in a word, anti-urban. A bias against cities, evident in contemporary public discourse, is a longstanding feature of the American political economy, and plays a central role in our tax code, major economic development programs, government purchasing, and other exercises of public power.

The Bias

In contrast to most developed capitalist nations, American public policy slights urban renters in favor of suburban homes, urban bus and subway riders in favor of suburban automobiles, and urban infrastructure in favor of ex-urban and rural development projects. Simultaneously, we do not require non-metro regions to pay the costs of maintaining the poor and dispossessed who are left behind by such acts of favoritism. Whether this anti-urbanism originated in genuine concern about leveling the wealth of different regions, or in racism, or in some misplaced notion that the happiest life was always found behind the wheel of an automobile, the general effect has been to artificially lower the costs--to individuals and firms--of living and working outside our metro regions, while artificially increasing the costs of living and working within them.

Though it is hard to calculate precisely, the subsidy to non-urban regions is on all counts considerable--annually, on the order of tens if not hundreds of billions. We have spent trillions building non-metro roads, but nowhere near that on metro ones or mass transit. Federal annual funding for mass transit has never been more than one-fifth of highway funding, and state ratios are even more unbalanced. The overwhelming share of federal and state economic development program support also goes to non-metro sites--more highways, sprawlsupporting infrastructure, exurban tax credits and low-interest loans for new development. Similarly, the deliberate siting of military bases and other government facilities outside cities or more developed regions has been and remains deliberate national policy.

So public policy substantially reduces the costs of living and investing outside metro areas, and thus encourages people to make those choices. But why should anyone object? Leave aside narrow questions of equity--why, for example, metro residents should be taxed, often regressively, for programs that hurt them. Leave aside aesthetic and cultural disagreements about whether city life is vibrant or merely vulgar. And assume, against all evidence, that suburbanites can insulate themselves from decaying urban cores. Are there any good reasons to oppose policies that have contributed to urban decline?

Why Care?

There are two reasons: one of political morality, the other of economics. As to political morality: lots of people live in cities and are likely to remain there; democracy is supposed to be "for the people"--all of them. With 130 million people in our urban areas, and 80 million (20 million of them children) in their declining central cities, anti-urban policies don't qualify. Furthermore, very large portions of this population are exceptionally poor, in receipt of exceptionally bad public services, and subject to exceptional violence. No one disputes the results--in high infant mortality, poor health, stunted development, shattered lives, and heavy grief.

On the economic side, anti-urbanism is very costly. For starters, sprawl and central- city degradation is wasteful. It wastes land, water, and energy, and squanders existing assets; as new houses, factories, and schools go up in the outer rings, perfectly good buildings, with established links to usable infrastructure, get boarded up further in. Take the excess costs on new construction and natural resources, add in the untimely depreciation of old capital stock, it's easily $300 billion in annual waste.

Then there are the economic costs of human neglect. Abandoning our central cities means forsaking the productive potential of their inhabitants while containing their resentment. The costs of containment are considerable, as ballooning budgets for new prisons and police make evident. And the opportunity costs of all that potential productivity are truly enormous. Forget about the hidden future Nobel Prize winners. Simply subtract the average lifetime earnings of those without decent health, education, or job access from those with these basic goods. Multiply by 80 million, or even 20. It's a big number--in the trillions--which translates into a lot of foregone tax revenue for the general population.

Furthermore, there is cost linkage. Many suburbanites are prepared to pay the costs and forego the benefits just mentioned as the price of their isolation. But that isolation is an illusion. Within regions, the economic fortunes of central cities and their suburbs, especially their inner-ring suburbs, are increasingly entwined. By the late 1980s, across a very wide range of metro regions, every $1,000 gained or lost in per capita city income was associated with a $690 gain or loss in per capita suburban income.2 Rotting central cities mean a poorer suburban future.

The really big cost, however, derives from the role that metro regions play in determining the pattern of national economic activity. Put baldly, revived urban regions are key to reversing the present stagnation in American living standards. This is a large claim: defending it will require that we step back briefly from the dynamics within metro regions and consider broader trends in the national economy and what is required to reverse them.

A High Road?

Despite all the talk about how American wages are now set in Beijing, adverse trends in American income (including income distribution) result today less from the downward pressures of international competition than from domestic policy choices.3 Specifically, we have made "low-road" strategies of response to new competitive pressures too easy and "high-road" strategies too hard. Low-road firms compete by keeping prices down, which means keeping costs down--beginning, typically, with wages. Applied across the economy, low-road strategies lead to sweated workers, economic insecurity, rising inequality, poisonous labor relations, and degraded natural environments. High-road firms focus on quality competition (with higher wages supported by customer willingness to pay for higher quality), require continual innovation in quality, and thus depend on more skilled and cooperative workers. Generalized, high-road strategies are associated with higher productivity, higher pay and better labor relations, reduced environmental damage, and greater firm commitment to the health and stability of surrounding human communities (needed to attract and keep skilled workers and managers).

Firms can make plenty of money on either path, but social gains are vastly greater on the high road. The principal political-economic failure of the past two decades--and it is political as much as economic--is that we have not done what we must to move the economy to it. Moving to the high road is associated with various transition costs, and staying on it depends on a variety of social supports. Those supports include effective educational and training institutions; better functioning labor markets, with fuller information about   requirements for job access and advancement; advanced   infrastructure of all kinds; modernization services and other   means of diffusing best manufacturing practice; and,   throughout, barriers to low-road defection. Because such   supports typically lie beyond the capacity of individual firms,   they need to be provided socially. We have not provided them.

Back to Metro

Here is where metro areas come in. Whatever their present difficulties, metropolitan economies are the natural base for a   high-road economy. To the extent that we now have any "highroad" production and service delivery in the United States, it is   already heavily concentrated in metropolitan regions.   Moreover, this correlation between metro regions and the   high-road strategy is no accident: a high-road strategy must be   a metro strategy because the high road requires the sheer   density of people and firms that is definitive of metro regions.

Metro density helps high-roading in three ways. First, density   facilitates worker organization by providing the proximity and   sheer numbers needed to support the infrastructure of new   organizing. Worker organization, in turn, directly helps to   close off the low road by obstructing its impulse to wagereduction. And worker organization helps pave the high road   too. Without the knowledge and cooperation of workers, firms   will find high-roading all but impossible--and both are easier   to secure if workers are organized and confident that they will   also benefit from increased quality and productivity.

Density also helps firms more directly. Economists, geographers, and economic development analysts use the concept of "agglomeration" to describe the benefits in skills,   productivity, and consumer access that result when particular   activities are concentrated in particular places. In addition,   firms in such regions don't just happen to be near each other   and share a regional labor market. They do business with each other in a way that connects them as if, in some ways, they were complementary plants of a single enterprise. Agglomerations are in turn associated with "increasing returns" on any given investment. When a single firm in one of these agglomerations improves its cost and quality performance, it creates a competitive advantage for the customers and suppliers in its cluster. Simply put, firms learn more and faster from each other.

Finally, density helps relieve the costs of providing the public goods (again, quality public education and training institutions, formal supports for cross-learning and upgrading among firms, integrated regional labor market services and worker credentialling systems, modern forms of transport, energy, water supplies, and communication linkages) on which such advanced production depends. It is much easier and cheaper to supply such goods with the human and material resources that density provides.

So here, in brief, is the argument: To combat further inequality and wage decline, we need to generalize a high-road competitive strategy. Getting firms to adopt and stick with that strategy will require a more demanding high-road frame for competition (closing off the low road) and a variety of specific supporting services and institutions (pavement for the high road). Neither can be supplied by individual firms acting alone. Density is the midwife to their achievement. And density means metro. A fair economic future, in short, depends on the viability of our urban areas.

How to Do It

But are metro regions really viable? What would it take to repeal the Iron Law, end the anti-urban bias of public policy, capture the natural advantages of density, and turn our policies more deliberately to building the infrastructure for high-road competition? Putting aside all-important questions of political will (we return to them later) and focusing for now on issues of public policy, the answer proceeds on two related tracks: we need a new array of policies for federal and state governments, and--coordinated with them--a new set for economic regions.

Track One

At the federal and state levels of government, the essential tasks are to keep states and communities from pursuing a competitive race to the bottom, raise minimum standards on firm performance, and get out of the way of the organizing needed to realize gains from cooperation. None of this need imply any new public expenditures. What it would mean is that federal and state governments would:

(1) Remove subsidies to low-roading firms. As an initial step, governments should announce that they will not award contracts or development grants to firms paying wages below some minimum level (say, sub-poverty

wages), or polluting above a certain level, or with a record of illegal resistance to worker organization. They should then move to mandate such standards generally, and gradually raise them. For example,

phasing in a massively increased minimum wage--say, to $10 an hour within 5 years--would do wonders for shutting down the low-road option and requiring firms to compete by improving quality. (Of course, there is no point urging firms onto a high road only to push them off a cliff. So this first element must be understood and treated as part of the larger project.)

(2) Discourage "bidding wars" between and within states. Governments often spend billions simply to lure business from one region to another, with no net gain for the national economy. One way to discourage this practice would be to tax any government bids at the next highest level of government (the federal government taxing the states, the states their local governments), or condition aid from those higher units on the lower one's participation in non-aggression pacts with colleagues. Of course, one region's "subsidy" is another's "investment for the future." So we need criteria to distinguish genuine investment that might also be expected to lure firms-for example, spending for better educational systems--from direct payoffs and abatements. But this task is not insurmountable, and even agreement on basic guidelines for the most extreme (if common) forms of current subsidies-e.g., those drawn through regressive taxes on people who are not aided by the resulting employment--would represent a big advance.

(3) Target development supports to regions on a per capita   basis. As a general rule of public policy, we should spend the   money where the people are, thus encouraging local   governments to increase density rather than avoid it. And let   the natural agglomerations of people and firms be rewarded by   letting them recapture their individual tax dollars for   collective self-improvement. Here too there are important   issues of design. We don't want incentives to agglomeration to be so intense as to encourage overcrowding or insupportable   population growth within regions. But the basic idea of   removing disincentives to otherwise naturally-occurring   agglomeration provides some guidance, and even modest   progress toward per capita equalization seems justified on   economic and social, as well as democratic grounds.

(4) Encourage the growth of economic development authorities on a functional, regional basis. While more than   half the population lives in what we've been calling metro   regions, only 6 percent is subject to any significant metro   governance. Moreover, the sheer number of sovereign subjurisdictions in these regions commonly poses formidable   barriers to planning. The Chicago metropolitan region, for   example, includes 265 separate municipalities, 1,200 separate   tax districts, and parts of six different mega-counties. State   and federal government could provide incentives for more   regional administrative structures--which are needed   minimally for basic infrastructure development--by making development aid and other supports by higher levels of government contingent on the development of such structures   lower down. In very few cases is there actual dispute about   what the boundaries of the regional

economy are: the problem   has been an absence of national or state leadership in fostering   regional frameworks for economic development and planning.

(5) Directly encourage high-roading. In all aspects of economic development spending, infrastructure support, pollution prevention and abatement programs, and the like,   reward regions or states that take the subsidiary policy steps   needed to move toward high-road production. Comparative   progress toward the high road is measurable. If measurable, it   should measured, with receipt of special federal monies   contingent on achieving progress. And, independent of what   the states do, the federal government should itself be much   more attentive to targeting its resources to encourage high-roading. It should target aid to integrated regions, clusters   within them, firms within those clusters. The lead federal   "manufacturing extension" agency--charged with upgrading   the performance of the small and medium-sized shops that   provide six of every ten manufacturing jobs--spends $100   million a year, and could reach literally tens of thousands of   small- and medium-sized manufacturers, already supplying (or trying to supply) to high-road clusters, if that money were   appropriately targeted on metro agglomerations.

Together, these five elements would work to remove the antiurban and low-road bias from contemporary state and federal   policy; they would encourage 18th- and 19th-century   jurisdictions to consider the realities of late 20th-century   regional economic dependence; and they would encourage   both firms and regions to exploit the advantages of density.

Track Two

Higher levels of government, however, can only do so much to   foster metro reconstruction. To be sure, moving the national   economy onto a high road would be of manifest national   benefit. But because a high road policy must be a metro   policy, regions themselves must play a large role in designing   and implementing it. What, then, should the regions do?

The short answer is that they need to break squarely with the   conventional economic development strategy (hereafter,   CEDS) still pursued by most cities and counties--the strategy   that lies behind the Iron Law of Decay--in favor of a high-road   project that takes full advantage of metro density. To fill out   this answer, lets distinguish CEDS and our alternative on five   dimensions.

(4) What Kind of Jobs? CEDS adapts to urban decline by promoting job growth without concern for the kind of jobs generated--which uusually means promoting low-wage jobs.   But low-wage jobs drag down wages elsewhere, encourage   further low-roading, eat away at the margin of struggling highroad firms, and draw on the tax base (the employers providing   them still need basic infrastructure, and the employees   occupying them still need basic services) without   proportionately contributing to it. Tax-base erosion, in turn,   leads to cutbacks in public goods and suburban flight: the Iron   Law again. Nevertheless, the strategy is perversely selfenforcing: as the city gets more squalid, desperation fuels the   view that jobs, any jobs at all, are what is needed, and the   thought

that the only alternative to low-wage employment is no employment at all.

A natural alternative is to direct dollars only to jobs of a certain kind, while building supports for them. Relying on a politics of opportunities and constraints, localities should make it easier for "good" employers to stay and expand-through the provision of a variety of services and opportunities for their improvement and competitiveness-- while making it harder for "bad" employers to do so--by insisting on certain standards on wages, pollution prevention, and so on. Such a policy could start by setting conditions on the receipt of government contracts and economic development supports and--especially supported by our new state and federal framework discouraging a "race to the bottom" between regions -- move to mandates on private activity.

(2) Attraction or Retention? CEDS focuses on attracting business rather than retaining and renewing the existing base of firms. It squanders one of the greatest assets of density, which is the natural grouping of similar firms--drawn together by the cross-learning, joint production, and other mutual support that proximity provides--in distinct industries or industry clusters. Mature metropolitan economies thrive when their core businesses upgrade, link to one another, or attract or spin off related enterprises that benefit from spatial proximity to existing industry leaders. But, as emphasized earlier, upgrading, networking, and incubating indigenous firms requires an infrastructure of support (technical assistance,

training, and the efficient supply of modern public goods). And while providing these is in the long run much more satisfying, in the short run it is easier to attract another Walmart. The principle become self-confirming as neglect of "the ones that brung ya" leads to decline in existing sources of wealth, making the attraction of new and different firms more compelling as an option.

Our alternative development strategy would focus on retention, renewal, upgrading, linkage, and incubation of existing firms--with local authorities investing in the infrastructure needed to realize gains from agglomeration. Through "early warning/early intervention" networks, they would recruit firms and workers to monitor the signs of distress in challenged firms, and develop the technical and financial intervention wherewithal to save jobs worth saving. At the same time, they would actively promote cross-firm learning and sectoral growth by encouraging firms to join together in marketing their products and training workers. And, drawing on the accumulated pension and other savings in the region, they would develop regional investment funds to support such intervention, increase community ownership of firms doing business there, and support promising spin-offs and incubation centers.

(3) Generic or Targeted Benefits? CEDS relies on generic tax abatements and other fiscal giveaways, rather than targeted breaks and regulation. Again, best evidence is that such enterprise zone-type development models simply do not work, and eventually erode the city's fiscal base. The jobs generated are seldom high-paying or

associated with significant capital   investment; the firms take the benefits and move on. In   contract, much evidence suggests that by a gradual tightening   of regulatory controls on production standards--whether minimum labor costs or emissions standards--business can be   encouraged to innovate in ways that improve both productivity   and the quality of community life. Doing this, however,   requires a willingness to impose significant costs on current   business, while insulating it from competition from noncomplying competitors. Most city governments have been   unwilling or unable to make this crucial step. The result,

however, is a race to the bottom among jurisdictions who offer escalating packages of sweeteners for investments firms   had already to decided to make.

Our alternative would set performance conditions on the receipt of public funds--tying subsidies to the achievement of   specific ends--and "claw back" those funds from firms that do   not meet the conditions. The more extensive the support from   the government and allied private institutions, of course, the   more extensive the demands that could reasonably be made on   the firms receiving it.

(4) What Role for Markets? CEDS sees greater public control   and accountability as bad for the economy, and it worries   when unions and community organizations put pressure on   economic policy. Starting from the largely correct perception   that government and the general public are ill-prepared to   instruct business on how best to achieve particular standards   or ends, it arrives at the incorrect conclusion that they are   incapable even of

specifying them.

But modern economies operate best when they can rely on a fair degree of public support for business goals--support best achieved when the public has significant say in setting those goals. And some associative action in the economy, including much that might be deemed "popular," is critical to the effective supply of the ingredients of advanced production. Design and construction of an effective training and credentialing system, for example, requires local knowledge of a variety of distinct productive settings and the ability to figure out policies that make sense across them. Confronting such issues, the state is commonly at a loss, as are individual firms. Unions and employer associations, with detailed knowledge across particular sites and the ability to compel

performance within them, are critical to success.

Building on these observations, our alternative would continue to let markets do what they do best--allocate scarce resources with some efficiency, and punish the noncompetitive--but would be unabashed in letting public authority and popular organizations to say something about what the goals of economic activity should be. And, breaking with "live free or die"/"private markets or public hierarchies" models of regulation, it would explicitly assign representative non-state institutions with local knowledge or other capacity not found in government itself (again, unions, employer organizations, community organizations) a role in economic administration. In our examples above, it might give substantial control over resources for skill training to sectoral   training consortia, or control of the early warning network to   responsible area unions.

(5) Public Goods? CEDS neglects the role that public goods   of many kinds--from the traditional "economic" ones of   transportation, technical assistance, and education and training   to the "social" ones of recreation, safety, and clean   environments--play in a local economy. In this, local economic   development efforts are behind the learning of most advanced   businesses, which rely on the economic goods for production   and the social goods to attract and retain a skilled workforce   and managerial personnel. Since no individual is able to   provide this economic and social infrastructure on its own, the decision about whether or not to provide it is among the most   crucial that local economic development authorities can make.   But the ability of such authorities to provide infrastructure   will depend directly on the population of high-roading firms   and associations with a stake in it: the failure to provide   decent infrastructure will drive that population down to the

point that authorities will only be able to attract low-road   firms seeking low-income markets and low-cost labor.

Instead of neglecting high-road infrastructure, our alternative   would build it. Sometimes this would mean serious   investment--as in effective transit systems connecting job   seekers to work throughout the region, or the provision of   training. More often than commonly thought, however, it   would simply mean fostering cooperation among existing   interests, or simply convening discussion of common   problems--among players who know what the problems are and collectively have the resources to solve many of them, but who heretofore have had no incentive or support from public authority in solving them together. In such situations government in effect says: "Here's a problem that we all know exists; you design a feasible solution accountable to the following values and show me how to pay for it; we will then pass a law making sure nobody defects from the necessary deal."

Consider the effects of systematically pursuing a program of this kind: the federal and state reforms, as well as the inversion of CEDS just described. Sprawl would be reduced, planning capacity would rise, wages would increase and inequalities decrease, neighborhoods would become less segregated and safer, public goods would be more abundant: democracy would more evidently show its contribution to the economy. And, as with any good strategy, it would be self-reenforcing: As subsidies to sprawl decrease, the attractions of metropolitan locations rise; as investment returns to metro cores, productivity within them increases, making higher wages more affordable; as organization of the real cluster basis of the economy proceeds, standards for job entry and advancement can be formalized and publicized, which helps to equalize wages; better wages secure the tax base; that helps pay for the expensive public goods which both further reduce inequality and attract high-roading firms; with more abundant public goods and better job access, central city residents look less "different," further promoting their hirability; and with greater regional power over something employers really want-skilled labor, infrastructure, technical assistance, credit--the ability of regions to discipline free-riders and defectors from common norms (e.g., on fair housing and hiring, land use, taxbase sharing) rises. In the limiting case, the economy actually   serves the people, rather than the people struggling to serve an   anonymous and immoral economy.

Who Can Do It?

But who could put all this together? And is it reasonable to   hope that they might?

Part of the answer is that it is happening already. Across the   country, you can find different pieces of the project we have   recommended. At least a few regions do have metropolitan   government, sensible planning policies, tax-base sharing   between rich and poor neighborhoods within the same region,   regional standards on zoning--including, critically, fair   housing policies that put poor minorities next to opportunity.   Many cities and counties, and some states, have passed "living   wage" or "anti-subsidy abuse" legislation putting enforceable conditions on receipt of public development monies. Many local planning and development departments have begun to   target their resources toward the improvement of existing   clusters of firms. And there are countless "visioning"   exercises--more or less effectively uniting diverse   communities within regions--to establish benchmarks on   regional performance and at least begin discussion of its   requisite infrastructure.

This said, these efforts remain exceptions; given continued low-roading competition, they are that much harder to sustain.   Nor, with the possible exception of Portland, is any one of   them truly comprehensive--putting the governance, planning,   finance, standards, supports, and popular organization pieces   together. Nor, to return to where we started, do any of them   enjoy appropriate support from the state and federal   governments. Very few of these efforts have, therefore, reached critical mass, tipping the dynamics of their regions. Still, the fact that so many initiatives are already in motion, from diverse quarters--some led by local government officials themselves, others by business, labor, community groups, or particular issue advocates--suggests a wide-ranging potential alliance out there, waiting to be organized. To appreciate its range, consider the different urban political forces--at each other's throats for so many years--who are now coming to recognize the limits of mutual antagonism.

The current scene pits labor against community, the employed against environmentalists, and central cities against the innerring, while obscuring relevant divisions within business, and letting the rich exurbs get off too cheap. But many of the mutual antagonists in this old politics are beginning to see an interest in alliance. White-dominated labor increasingly recognizes that its declining city membership no longer suffices to protect it against low wage privatization and the destruction of regional labor market standards, let alone assure the public investments needed to support highwage production and services. It needs the voting support of (heavily disorganized) central city Black, Latino, and Asian populations: to get that support, it will need fully to open itself to them. Those populations, in turn, know that their economic devastation will not be reversed anytime soon through an increased welfare effort or expanded public sector. They need private sector investment and jobs within their communities, and access to jobs without, and they need those jobs to pay a living wage. And increasingly they recognize that these things are more likely achieved if they are allied with unions.

Environmentalists and those concerned about organization inside firms, meanwhile, are finding common ground on the   supplyside of production. Just as unions have found that they   can only defend member interests by getting involved in   decisions about technology, product strategy, investment, and   work organization, environmentalists recognize that moving   from pollution abatement to sourcereduction requires a   presence inside the firm. Innerring suburbanites, whose kids   are also joining gangs, and who are in many cases losing   employment at faster rates than the central cities, are waking   to the fact that the same lowwage sprawl that has almost   destroyed the central cities is now destroying them. And both central and inner-ring recognize their common interest in getting the rich suburbs to carry their share of regional burdens. Finally, metro business itself, at least that part of it   that cannot easily flee (for example, because of existing collective bargaining agreements, or pension obligations, or   heavy sunk investment in plant and equipment), is interested,   like any good business, in limiting competition to itself,   interested in particular in eliminating the low-roaders now   taking away their margins.

Put these forces together in any metro region--and the program outlined here has a real chance of benefiting all of   them--and you have a powerful political coalition.

Again, we're only talking about what we might reasonably hope for. As with any good, lots of obstacles might obstruct its   achievement. But material interest strongly supports this grand   coalition. And recent experience in mobilizing directly on that   interest--be it the grassroots Campaign for a Sustainable   Milwaukee, or legislative efforts at more tax-base sharing in   the Twin Cities, or the more business-led efforts in Louisville   or Cleveland--suggest the possibilities of real movement. What is most urgently needed are some enterprising politicians, labor leaders, savvy community organizers, or sensible metro businesspeople to get in front of a parade that's

waiting to form.

And if people get organized, elected officials can be made to   follow. In getting the relevant state and federal policy supports, the gravamen of success is simply stated: an alliance   of the city and inner-ring suburban delegations--still, in   combination, a clear majority in Congress and most state   legislatures--to press the general interest against recalcitrant   rich suburbanites and low-road firms. If the general interest   doesn't move those delegations, the fact that their respective   constituencies are getting unfairly and jointly savaged should.   Someone should invite our currently divided metro officials   into a room together, show them a few numbers, and point to the large mixed crowd of constituents preparing to march outside.

ENDING
THE
DIGITAL
DIVIDE

5. Assess workforce training needs involving information technologies, develop curricula, train current and prospective   employees, and help employees gain experience in applying the   technical skills they have acquired through training.

6. Expand resources for employees to participate in training   programs through scholarships or low interest loans, or time   off for those participating in training.

7. Tap into nontraditional labor pools, including older workers, minorities, women, and recent college graduates   trained in non-IT disciplines.

8. Fund and support programs to relieve pressure on post   secondary workforce development teaching infrastructures,

 including the development of strategies to recruit faculty,   retain them, and maintain their current skills.

5. Encourage technical workers to become involved in local   school systems by providing time off during working hours to   teach, mentor, or work with students.

6. Increase on-the-job training and form industry/union/education/community partnerships to expand   workforce development and training at all levels.

7. Join   together   to   help   under-represented   groups, especially in   low income   and   rural   communities, to overcome entry barriers   to   good   paying   jobs, including those in IT labor markets.

The Future
of Public
Educatio
n

In the past two years, the number of students expelled from elementary and secondary schools in Chicago has nearly doubled. Expelled kids get sent to something called "safe schools," run by for-profit organizations. When a reporter asked Chicago officials why the number of spaces in the forprofit academies was far smaller than the number of expelled students, the reporter was reassured. Not to worry. They donÆt all show up. Meanwhile, the city is writing new   categories and new zero-tolerance policies to push reform   along. Chicago is the home of get-tough reform, and all these   changes have been made in the name of upgrading "standards."   The results? Test scores over the past three years have risen,   we are told, by 3.4 percent in Chicago. ThatÆs a few more   right answers on a standardized test, maybe.

Back in my home state, Massachusetts, the town of Lynnfield announced that it was time to end METCO, a program that for twenty years brought minority children into nearly all-white, middle-class, suburban communities. The Board members explained to the press that the program wasnÆt helping the Lynnfield schools raise their "standards"-that is, their scores on the new tough state tests. Sometimes equity and excellence just donÆt mix well. So sorry.1 The stories of Chicago and Lynnfield capture a dark side of the "standards-based reform" movement in American education: the politically popular movement to devise national or statemandated standards for what all kids should know, and highstakes tests and sanctions to make sure they all know it. The stories show how the appeal to standards can mask and make way for other agendas: punishing kids, privatizing public education, giving up on equity.

I know how advocates of the movement to standardize standards will respond: "Good reform ideas can always be misused. Our proposals are designed to help kids, save public education, and ensure equity."

I disagree. Even in the hands of sincere allies of children, equity, and public education, the current push for far greater standardization than we ever previously attempted is fundamentally misguided. It will not help to develop young minds, contribute to a robust democratic life, or aid the most vulnerable of our fellow citizens. By shifting the locus of authority to outside bodies, it undermines the capacity of schools to instruct by example in the qualities of mind that schools in a democracy should be fostering in kidsresponsibility for one's own ideas, tolerance for the ideas of others, and a capacity to negotiate differences. Standardization instead turns teachers and parents into the local instruments of externally imposed expert judgment. It thus decreases the chances that young people will grow up in the midst of adults who are making hard decisions and exercising mature

judgment in the face of disagreements. And it squeezes out those schools and educators that seek to show alternate possibilities, to explore other paths.

The standardization movement is not based on a simple mistake. It rests on deep assumptions about the goals of education and the proper exercise of authority in the making of decisions- assumptions we ought to reject in favor of a different vision of a healthy democratic society. Drawing on my experience in schools in New York City and Boston, I show that this alternative vision isnÆt utopian, even if it might be messy-as democracy is always messy.

Standards-Based Reform

Standards-based reform systems vary enormously in their details. But they are generally organized around a set of four interconnected mechanisms: first, an official document (sometimes called a framework) designed by experts in various fields that describes what kids should know and be able to do at given grade levels in different subjects; second, classroom curricula-commercial textbooks and scripted programs-that are expected to convey that agreed-upon knowledge; third, a set of assessment tools (tests) to measure whether children have achieved the goals specified in the framework; and fourth, a scheme of rewards and penalties directed at schools and school systems, but ultimately at individual kids, who fail to meet the standards as measured by the tests. Cut-off points are set at various politically feasible points-in some states they are pegged so that nearly 90 percent of the students fail whereas others fail less than 10 percent. School administrators (and possibly teachers) are fired if schools fail to reach particular goals after a given period of time, and kids are held back in grade, sent to summer school, and finally refused diplomas if they donÆt meet the cut-off scores.

Massachusetts, for instance, has recently devised tests in English, mathematics, history, and science (to be followed by other subjects over time) covering the stateÆs mandated frameworks. The tests are given in grades four, eight, and ten. Beginning in 2003, students will need to pass the grade-ten tests to get a Massachusetts high school diploma; moreover, the tests are intended to serve as the sole criteria for rating   schools, for admission to public colleges, and for as many   other rewards and sanctions as busy state officials can devise. The Massachusetts tests are not typical, but then each state has its own variant. The Massachusetts tests are unusually long (fifteen to twenty hours), and cover a startling amount of material. For fourth graders the history and social studies portions allow the test makers to ask questions about anything   that happened between prehistoric times and 500 AD in "the   world," and in the United States until 1865. While world   history expands in the upper grades, you can get a high school   diploma without ever studying US history after 1865. The   science and math portions are equally an inch deep and a mile   wide. And the selections and questions on the reading tests   were initially designed with full knowledge (and intent) that, if   scores do not immediately improve, eighty percent of all   fourth graders would fail-even though Massachusetts fourth   graders rank near the top in most national reading assessments. But the specifics of the tests are not the central issue. Even if they were replaced by saner instruments, they would still embody a fundamentally misguided approach to school reform. To see just how they are misguided, we need first to   ask about their rationale. Why are these tests being imposed?

Why Standards?

Six basic assumptions underlie the current state and national   standard setting and testing programs now off the ground in   49 of 50 states (all but Iowa):

5. Goals:It is possible and desirable to agree on a single definition of what constitutes a well-educated 18-year-old and   demand that every school be held to the same definition. We   have, it is argued, gotten by without such an agreement at a   great cost-witness the decline of public education-in   comparison to other nations with tight national systems.

6. Authority: The task of defining "well-educated" is best left   to experts-educators, political officials, leaders from industry   and the major academic disciplines-operating within a system   of political checks and balances. That each stateÆs definition   at the present time varies so widely suggests the eventual need for a single national standard.

3. Assessment: With a single definition in place, it will be   possible to measure and compare individuals and schools   across communities-local, state, national, international. To   this end, curricular norms for specific ages and grades should   be translated into objective tests that provide a system of   uniform scores for all public, and if possible private, schools   and districts. Such scores should permit public comparisons   between and among students, schools, districts, and states at   any point in time.

4. Enforcement: Sanctions, too, need to be standardized, thus   removed from local self-interested parties-including parents,   teachers, and local boards. Only a more centralized and distant   system can resist the pressures from people closest to the   child-the very people who have become accustomed to low   standards.

5. Equity: Expert-designed standards, imposed through tests,   are the best way to achieve educational equity. While a   uniform national system would work best if all students had   relatively equal resources, equity requires introducing such a   system as rapidly as possible regardless of disparities. It is   especially important for schools with scarcer resources to   focus their work, concentrating on the essentials.   Standardization with remotely controlled sanctions thus offers   the best chance precisely for underfunded communities and schools, and for less well-educated and less powerful families.

6. Effective Learning: Clear-cut expectations, accompanied by   automatic rewards and punishments, will produce greater   effort, and effort-whether induced by the desire for rewards,   fear of punishment, or shame-is the key to learning. When   teachers as well as students know what constitutes failure, and

also know the consequences of failure, a rational system of   rewards and punishments becomes an effective tool. Automatic penalties work for schooling much as they do for   crime and punishment: consistency and certainty are the keys.   For that reason compassion requires us to stand firm, even in   the face of pain and failure in the early years.

A Crisis?

The current standards-based reform movement took off in 1983 in response to the widely held view that America was at extreme economic risk, largely because of bad schools. The battle cry-called out first in A Nation At Risk-launched an attack on dumb teachers, uncaring mothers, social promotion, and general academic permissiveness. Teachers and a new group labeled "educationists" were declared the main enemy, thus undermining their credibility, and setting the stage for cutting them and their concerns out of the cure. According to critics, American education needed to be reimagined, made more rigorous, and, above all, brought under the control of experts who-unlike educators and parents-understood the new demands of our economy and culture. The cure might curtail the work of some star teachers and star schools, and it might lead, as the education chief of Massachusetts recently noted, to a lot of crying fourth graders. But the gravity of the long-range risks to the nation demanded strong medicine.

Two claims were thus made: that our once-great public system was no longer performing well, and that its weaknesses were undermining AmericaÆs economy.

Most critics have long agreed that the data in support of the claim about school decline are at best weak (see Richard Rothstein's 1998 book, The Way We Were?). As a result, the debate shifted-although the average media story hardly noticed-to an acknowledgement that even if there was not a decline in school achievement, the demands of the new international economy required reinventing our schools anyway. Whether the crisis was real or imagined, change was required. But efforts to induce changes in teaching and learning met with widespread resistance from many different quarters-from citizens, parents, teachers, and local officials. Some schools changed dramatically, and some changed bits and pieces, but the timetable was far too slow for the reformers.

The constituents who originally coalesced around A Nation at Risk began to argue that the fault lay either in the nature of public schooling itself or in the excesses of local empowerment. The cure would have to combine more competition from the private or semi-private sector and more rigorous control by external experts who understood the demands of our economy and had the clout to impose change. This latter viewpoint has dominated the standards-based reform movement.

Unfortunately, a sense of reality has been lost in these shifting terms of debate. Now, fifteen years after analysts discovered the great crisis of American education, the American economy is soaring, the productivity of our workforce is probably tops in the world, and our system of advanced education is the envy of the world. In elementary school literacy (where critics claim that sentimental pedagogues have for decades failed to teach children how to read), the United States still ranks second or third, topped only by one or another of the Scandinavian countries. While we rank lower in math and science tests, we continue to lead the world in technology and inventiveness. If the earlier argument was right and economic prowess requires   good schooling, then teachers in America ought to be   congratulated, and someone should be embarrassed by the   false alarm. Instead, the idea that schools are a disaster, and   that fixing them fast is vital to our economy, has become   something of a truism. It remains the excuse for all reform

efforts, and for carrying them out on the scale and pace   proposed.

Educators from the Progressive tradition are often accused of   "experimenting" on kids. But never in the history of the nation   have Progressives proposed an experiment so drastic, vast, and   potentially serious in its real-life impact on millions of young   people. If the consequences are other than those its supporters   hope for, the harm to the nationÆs educational system and the   youngsters involved-maybe even to our economy-will be large   and hard to undo.

The Real Crisis

The coalition of experts which produced A Nation at Risk were wrong when they announced the failure of American public education and its critical role in our economic decline. Constructive debate about reform should begin by acknowledging this misjudgment. But it should then also acknowledge the even bigger crisis that schools have played a major part in deepening, if not actually creating, and could play a big part in curing. This crisis requires quite a different set of responses, often in direct conflict with standardization.

An understanding of this other crisis begins by noting that we have the lowest voter turnout by far of any modern industrial country; we are exceptional for the absence of responsible care for our most vulnerable citizens (we spend less on child welfare-baby care, medical care, family leave-than almost every competitor); we don't come close to our competitors in income equity; and our high rate of (and investment in) incarceration places us in a class by ourselves. All of these, of course, effect some citizens far more than others: and the heaviest burdens fall on the poor, the young, and people of color.

These social and political indicators are suggestive of a crisis in human relationships. Virtually all discussions-right or leftabout what's wrong in our otherwise successful society acknowledge the absence of a sense of responsibility for one's community and of decency in personal relationships. An important cause of this subtler crisis, I submit, is that the closer our youth come to adulthood the less they belong to communities that include responsible adults, and the more stuck they are in peer-only subcultures. We have created two parallel cultures, and it's no wonder the ones on the grown-up side are feeling angry at the way the ones on the other side live and act: apparently foot-loose and fancy-free but in truth often lost, confused, and knit-together for temporary self-protection. The consequences are critical for all our youngsters, but obviously more severe-often disastrous-for those less identified with the larger culture of success.

Many changes in our society aided and abetted the shifts that have produced this alienation. But one important change has been in the nature of schooling. Our schools have grown too distant, too big, too standardized, too uniform, too divorced from their communities, too alienating of young from old and old from young. Few youngsters and few teachers have an opportunity to know each other by more than name (if that); and schools are organized so as to make "knowing each other" nearly impossible. In such settings itÆs hard to teach young people how to be responsible to others, or to concern themselves with their community. At best they develop loyalties to the members of their immediate circle of friends (and perhaps their own nuclear family). Even when they take on teen jobs their fellow workers and their customers are likely to be peers. Apprenticeship as a way to learn to be an adult is disappearing. The public and its schools, the "real" world and the schoolhouse, young people and adults have become disconnected, and until they are reconnected no list of particular bits of knowledge will be of much use.

In my youth there were over 200,000 School Boards. Today there are fewer than 20,000, and the average school, which in my youth had only a few hundred students, now holds thousands. As I write, Miami and Los Angeles are in the process of building the two largest high schools ever. The largest districts and the largest and most anonymous schools

are again those that serve our least advantaged children.

Because of the disconnection between the public and its schools, the power to protect or support them now lies increasingly in the hands of public or private bodies that have no immediate stake in the daily life of the students. CEOs, federal and state legislators, university experts, presidential think tanks make more and more of the daily decisions about schools. For example, the details of the school day and year are determined by state legislators-often down to minutes per day for each subject taught, and whether to promote Johnny from third to fourth grade. The school's budget depends on it. Site-based school councils are increasingly the "in" thing, just as the scope of their responsibility narrows.

Public schools, after a romance with local power-beginning in the late 1960s and ending in the early 1990s-are increasingly organized as interchangeable units of a larger state organism, each expected to conform to the intelligence of some central agency or expert authority. The locus of authority in young peopleÆs lives has shifted away from the adults kids know well and who know the kids well-at a cost. Home schooling or private schooling seem more and more the natural next step for those with the means to do so and the desire to remain in authority.

Our school troubles are not primarily due to too-easy coursework or too much tolerance for violence. The big trouble lies instead in the company our children keep-or, more   precisely, don't keep. They no longer keep company with usthe grown-ups they are about to become. And the adults they   do encounter seem less and less worthy of their respect. What   kid, after all, wants to be seen emulating people heÆs been   told are too dumb to exercise power, and are simply

implementing the commands of the real experts?

Alternative Assumptions

Just as the conventional policy assumptions emerge naturally from a falsely diagnosed crisis, so does the crisis I have sketched suggest an alternative set of assumptions.

3. Goals: In a democracy, there are multiple, legitimate definitions of "a good education" and "well-educated," and it is desirable to acknowledge that plurality. Openly differing viewpoints constitute a healthy tension in a democratic, pluralistic society. Even where a mainstream view exists, alternate views that challenge the consensus are critical to the society's health. Young people need to be exposed to competing views, and to adults debating choices about what's most important.

As John Stuart Mill said, "It is not the mind of heretics that are deteriorated most, by the ban placed on all inquiry which does not end in the orthodox conclusions. The greatest harm is done to those who are not heretics, and whose whole mental development is cramped, and their reason cowed, by the fear of heresy."

4. Authority: In fundamental questions of education, experts should be subservient to citizens. Experts and laymen alike have an essential role in shaping both ends and means, the what and the how. While it is wise to involve experts from both business and the academy, they provide only one set of opinions, and are themselves rarely of a single mind. Moreover, it is educationally important for young people to be in the

company of adults-teachers, family members, and other adults in their own communities-powerful enough to decide   important things. They need to witness the exercise of

 judgment, the weighing of means and ends by people they can   imagine becoming; and they need to see how responsible   adults handle disagreement. If we think the adults in children's   lives are, in Jefferson's words, "not enlightened enough to   exercise their control with a wholesome discretion, the remedy   is not to take it from them, but to inform their discretion by   education."

3. Assessment: Standardized tests are too simple and simpleminded for high stakes assessment of children and schools.   Important decisions regarding kids and teachers should always   be based on multiple sources of evidence that seem   appropriate and credible to those most concerned. These are   old testing truisms, backed even by the testing industry, which   has never claimed the level of omniscience many standards   advocates assume of it. The state should only require that   forms of assessment be public, constitutionally sound, and   subject to a variety of "second opinions" by experts   representing other interested parties. Where states feel obliged   to set norms-for example, in granting state diplomas or access to state universities-these should be flexible, allowing schools   maximum autonomy to demonstrate the ways they have   reached such norms through other forms of assessment.

4. Enforcement: Sanctions should remain in the hands of the   local community, to be determined by people who

know the   particulars of each child and each situation. The power of both   business and the academy are already substantial; their access   to the means of persuasion (television, the press, etc.) and   their power to determine access to jobs and higher education   already impinge on the freedom of local communities.   Children, their families, and their communities should not be   required to make decisions about their own students and their own work based on such external measures. It is sufficient that

they are obliged to take them into account in their   deliberations about their childrenÆs future options.

5. Equity: A more fair distribution of resources is the principal   means for achieving educational equity. The primary national   responsibility is to narrow the resource gap between the most   and least advantaged, both between 9 a.m. and 3 p.m. and   during the other five-sixths of their waking lives, when rich   and poor students are also learning-but very different things.   To this end publicly accessible comparisons of educational   achievement should always include information regarding the   relative resources that the families of students, schools, and communities bring to the schooling enterprise.

6. Effective Learning: Improved learning is best achieved by   improving teaching and learning relationships, by enlisting the   energies of both teachers and learners. The kinds of learning   required of citizens cannot be accomplished by standardized   and centrally imposed systems of learning, even if we desired   it for other reasons. Human learning, to be efficient, effective,   and

long-lasting, requires the engagement of learners on their own behalf, and rests on the relationships that develop between schools and their communities, between teachers and   their students, and between the individual learner and what is   to be learned.

No "scientific" argument can conclusively determine whether   this set of assumptions or the set sketched earlier is true.   Although some research suggests that human learning is less   efficient when motivated by rewards and punishments, and that   fear is a poor motivator, I doubt that further research will   settle the issue. But because of the crisis of human   relationships, I urge that we consider the contrary claims more   seriously than we have. We may even find that in the absence   of strong human relationships rigorous intellectual training in   the most fundamental academic subjects canÆt flourish. In a world shaped by centralized media, restoring a greater balance   of power between local communities and central authorities,   between institutions subject to democratic control and those   beyond their control, may be vastly more important than   educational reformers bent on increased centralization   acknowledge.

An Alternative Model

Suppose, then, that we think about school reform in light of these alternative assumptions. What practical model of schools and learning do they support? In brief, our hope lies in   schools that are more personal, compelling, and attractive than   the internet or TV, where youngsters can keep company with   interesting and powerful adults, who are in turn in alliance   with the studentsÆ families and local institutions. We need to   surround kids with adults who know and care for our children,   who have opinions and are accustomed to expressing them   publicly, and who know how to reach reasonable collective   decisions in the face of disagreement. That means increasing   local decision-making, and simultaneously decreasing the size and bureaucratic complexity of schools. Correspondingly, the   worst thing we can do is to turn teachers and schools into the   vehicles for implementing externally- imposed standards.

Is such an alternative practical? Are the assumptions behind it   mere sentiment?

At the Mission Hill in Boston, one of ten new Boston public   schools initiated by the Boston Public Schools and the Boston   Teachers Union, we designed a school to support such   alternative practices. The families that came to Mission Hill   were chosen by lottery and represent a cross-section of   Boston's population. We intentionally kept the school smallless than 200 students ages five to thirteen-so that the adults   could meet regularly, take responsibility for each others work, and argue over how best to get things right. Parents join the staff not only for formal governance meetings, but for monthly informal suppers, conversations, good times. Our oldest kids-the eighth graders-will graduate only when they can show us all that they meet our graduation standards, which are the result of lots of parent, staff, and community dialogue over several years.

All our students study-once when they are little, once when they are older-a school-wide interdisciplinary curriculum. Last fall they all became experts on Boston and Mission Hill, learning its history (and their own), geography, architecture, distinct neighborhoods, and figures of importance. Last winter they all recreated ancient Egypt at 67 Allegheny Street. This coming winter they will recreate ancient China. Each spring they dig into a science-focused curriculum theme. The common curriculum allowed us, for example, to afford professional and amateur Egyptologists who joined us from time to time as lively witnesses to a life-long passion. We have a big central corridor which serves as our public mall, where kids paint murals, mix together to read, and talk across ages. High school students, who share the building with us, read with little ones, take them on trips, and generally model what it can mean to be a more responsible and well-educated person.

We invented our own standards-not out of whole cloth but with an eye to what the world out there expects and what we deem valuable and important. And we assessed them through the work the kids do and the commentary of others about that work. Our standards are intended to deepen and broaden young people's habits of mind, their craftsmanship, and their work   habits. Other schools may select quite a different way of   describing and exhibiting their standards. But they too need to   consciously construct their standards in ways that give   schooling purpose and coherence, and then commit themselves   to achieving them. And the kids need to understand the standards and their rationale. They must see school as not just   a place to get a certificate, but a place that lives by the same standards it sets for them. Thus the Mission Hill school not   only sets standards but has considerable freedom and   flexibility with regard to how it spends its public funds and   organizes its time to attain them. All ten pilot schools offer   examples of different ways this might play out, ways that   could be replicated in all Boston schools.

Standards of assessment are not once-for-all issues. We reexamine our school constantly to see that it remains a place   that engages all of us in tough but interesting learning tasks,   nourishes and encourages the development of reasonable and   judicious trust, and nurtures a passion for making sense of   things and the skills needed to do so. We expect disagreements-sometimes painful ones. We know that even well-intentioned, reasonable people cross swords over deeply   held beliefs. But we know, too, that these differences can be   sources of valuable education when the school itself can   negotiate the needed compromises.

What is impressive at Mission Hill, in the other Pilot schools,   at the Central Park East Schools in New YorkÆs East Harlem   (where I worked for 25 years), and the thousands of other   small schools like them, is that over time the kids buy in.   These schools receive the same per capita public funding as   other schools, are subject to city and state testing, and must   obey the same basic health, safety, and civil rights regulations.   But because these schools are small, the families and faculties   are together by choice, and all concerned can exercise   substantial power over staffing, scheduling, curriculum, and assessment, the schools' cultural norms and expectations are   very different than most other public schools.

The evidence suggests that most youngsters have a sufficiently   deep hunger for the relationships these schools offer themamong kids and between adults and kids-that they choose it   over the alternative cultures on the Net, tube, and street. Over   ninety percent of Central Park East's very typical students   stuck it out, graduated, and went on to college. And most   persevered through higher education. Did they ever rebel, get   mad at us, reassert their contrary values and adolescent   preferences? Of course. Did we fail with some? Yes. But it   turns out that the hunger for grown-up connections is strong enough to make a difference, if we give it a chance. Studies   conducted on the other similar schools launched in New York   between 1975 and 1995 showed the same pattern of success.

Standards, yes. Absolutely. But as Ted Sizer, who put the idea   of standards on the map in the early 1980s, also told us then: we need standards held by real people who matter in the lives   of our young. School, family, and community must forge their   own, in dialogue with and in response to the larger world of   which they are a part. There will always be tensions, but if the   decisive, authoritative voice always comes from anonymous outsiders, then kids cannot learn what it takes to develop their   own voice.

I know this "can be" because I have been there. The flowering   of so many new public schools of choice over the past two   decades proves that under widely different circumstances, very   different kinds of leadership and different auspices, a powerful   alternative to externally-imposed standards is available.

But I also know the powerful reasons why it "can not be"-because I have witnessed first-hand the resistance to allowing   others to follow suit, much less encouraging or mandating   them to do so. The resistance comes not simply from bad   bureaucrats or fearful unions (the usual bogeymen), but   legislators and mayors and voters, from citizens who think that   anything public must be all things to all constituents   (characterless and mediocre by definition), and from various   elites who see teachers and private citizens as too dumb to   engage in making important decisions. That's a heady list of   resisters.

But small self-governing schools of choice-operating with considerable flexibility and freedom-also resonate with large   numbers of people, including many of those who are gathering   around charter schools, and even some supporters of   privatization and home schooling. They too come from a wide   political spectrum and could be mobilized.

Accountability

And yet doubts about accountability will linger. In a world of smaller, more autonomous schools not responsible to centralized standards, how will we know who is doing a good job and who is not? How can we prevent schools from claiming they are doing just fine (and being believed), when it may not be true? Are we simply forced to trust them, with no independent evidence?

What lies behind these worries? For those who accept the conventional assumptions, anything but top-down standardization seems pointless. But for those whose concern is more practical there are some straightforward answers to the issue of accountability that do not require standardization.

To begin with, I am not advocating the elimination of all systems for taking account of how schools and students are doing. In any case, that is hardly a danger. Americans invented the modern, standardized, norm-referenced test. Our students have been taking more tests, more often, than any nation on the face of the earth, and schools and districts have been going public with test scores starting almost from the moment children enter school. By third or fourth grade (long before any of our international competitors bother to test children) we have test data for virtually all schools-by race, class, and gender. We know exactly how many kids did better or worse in each and every subcategory. We have test data for almost every grade thereafter in reading and math, and to some degree in all other subjects. This has been the case for nearly half a century. Large numbers of our eighteen-year-olds now take standardized college entry tests (SATs and ACTs). In addition, the national government now offers us its own tests-the

NAEP-which are given to an uncontaminated sample of students from across the United States and now reported by grade and state. And all of the above is very public.

In addition, public schools have been required to produce statements attesting to their financial integrity-how they spend their money-at least as rigorously as any business enterprise. They are held accountable for regularly reporting who works for them and what their salaries are. In most systems there are tightly prescribed rules and regulations; schools are obliged to fill out innumerable forms regarding almost every aspect of their work-how many kids are receiving special education, how many incidents of violence, how many suspensions, how many graduates, what grades students have received, how many hours and minutes they study each and every subject, and the credentials of their faculties. This information, and much more, is public. And the hiring and firing of superintendents has become a very common phenomenon.

In a nation in which textbooks are the primary vehicle for distributing school knowledge, a few major textbook publishers, based on a few major state textbook laws, dominate the field, offering most teachers, schools, and students very standardized accounts of what is to be learned, and when and how to deliver this knowledge. Moreover, most textbooks have always come armed with their own end-ofchapter tests, increasingly designed to look like the real thing;   indeed, test makers also are the publishers of many of the   major standardized tests.

In short, we have been awash in accountability and standardization for a very long time. What we are missing is   precisely the qualities that the last big wave of reform was   intended to respond to: teachers, kids, and families who

donÆt know each other or each others work and don't take responsibility for it. We are missing communities built around   their own articulated and public standards and ready to show   them off to others.

The schools I have worked in and support have shown how   much more powerful accountability becomes when one takes   this latter path. The work produced by Central Park East   students, for example, is collected regularly in portfolios; it is   examined (and in the case of high school students, judged) by   tough internal and external reviewers, in a process that closely   resembles a doctoral dissertation oral exam. The standards by   which a student is judged are easily accessible to families,   clear to kids, and capable of being judged by other parties. In   addition such schools undergo school-wide external   assessments which take into account the quality of their   curriculum, instruction, staff development, and culture as well   as the impact of the school on studentÆs future success (in college, work, etc.).

Are the approaches designed by Central Park East or Mission   Hill the best way? ThatÆs probably the wrong question. We   never intended to suggest that everyone should follow our   system. It would be nice if it were easier for others to adopt   our approach, but it would be even better if it were easier-in   fact required-that others adopt alternatives to it, including the   use of standardized tests if they so choose. My argument is for   more local control, not for one true way.

I opt for more local control not because I think the larger society has no common interests at stake in how we educate   all children, nor because local people are smarter or   intrinsically more honorable. Of course not. The interests of   wider publics are important in my way of thinking. I know that   pressure exists at Mission Hill not to accept or push out   students who are difficult to educate, who will make us look   worse on any test, or whose families are a nuisance. ItÆs a   good thing that others are watching us to prevent such

exclusion.

But in 1999, the United States is hardly in danger of too much   localized power in education. (The only local powers we seem   to be interested in expanding are those that allow us to resegregate our schools by race or gender.) What is missing is   balance-some power in the hands of those whose agenda is   first and foremost the feelings of particular kids, their   particular families, their perceived local values and needs.   Without such balance my knowledge that holding David over   in third grade will not produce the desired effects is useless   knowledge. Neither is my knowledge of different ways to   reach him through literature or history. This absence of local   power is bad for DavidÆs education and bad for democracy. A   back-seat driver may know more than the actual driver, but there are limits to what can be accomplished from the rear seat.

In short, the argument is not about the need for standards or   accountability, but about what kind serves us best. I believe   standardization will make it harder to hold people accountable   and harder to develop sound and useful standards. The   intellectual demands of the 21st century, as well as the   demands of democratic life, are best met by preserving plural   definitions of a good education, local decision-making, and   respect for ordinary human judgments.

Education and Democracy

If we are to make use of what we knew in Dewey's day (and know even better today) about how the human species best learns, we will have to start by throwing away the dystopia of the ant colony, the smoothly functioning (and quietly humming) factory where everything goes according to plan, and replace it with a messy, often rambunctious, community, with its multiple demands and complicated trade-offs. The new schools that might better serve democracy and the economy will have to be capable of constantly remaking themselves and still provide for sufficient stability, routine, ritual, and shared ethos. Impossible? Of course.

So such schools will veer too far one way or the other at different times in their history, will learn from each other, shift focus, and find a new balance. There will always be a party of order and a party of messiness.

But if schools are not all required to follow all the same fads, maybe they will learn something from their separate experiments. And that will help to nurture the two indispensable traits of a democratic society: a high degree of tolerance for others, indeed genuine empathy for them, and a high degree of tolerance for uncertainty, ambiguity, and puzzlement, indeed enjoyment of them.

A vibrant and nurturing community, with clear and regular guideposts-its own set of understandings, and a commitment to each other that feels something rather like love and affection-can sustain such rapid change without losing its humanity. Such a community must relish its disagreements, its oddballs, its misfits. Not quite families, but closer to our definition of family than factory, such schools will make high demands on their members, have a sustaining and relentless sense of purpose and coherence, but be ready also to always (at least sometimes) even reconsider their own core beliefs. We will come home exhausted, but not burned out. Everything that moves us toward these qualities will be good for the ideal of democracy. A democracy in which less than half its members see themselves as "making enough difference" to bother to vote in any election is surely endangered-far more endangered, at risk, than our economy. It's for the loss of belief in the capacity to influence the world, not our economic ups and downs, that we educators should accept some responsibility. What I have learned from thirty years in small powerful schools is that it is here above all that schools can make a difference, that they can alter the odds. We canÆt beat the statistical advantage on the next round of tests that being advantaged has over being disadvantaged; we can, however, substantially affect the gap between rich and poor where it will count, in the long haul of life. Even there itÆs hard to see how schools by themselves can eliminate the gap, but we can stop enlarging it. The factory-like schools we invented a century ago to handle the masses were bound to enlarge the gap. But trained mindlessness at least fit the world of work so many young people were destined for. We seem now to be reinventing a 21st century version of the factorylike school-for the mind-workers of tomorrow.

It is a matter of choice-such a future does not roll in on the

wheels of inevitability. We have the resources, the

knowledge, and plenty of living examples of the many different kinds of schools that might serve our needs better. All we need is a little more patient confidence in the good sense of "the people"-in short, a little more commitment to democracy.

A HOUSING CRISIS

Saving America's Affordable Rental Housing Stock:
The   Crisis, and the Appropriate Financial Services
Role

Losing Ground: Why We Need to Preserve Affordable
Housing   The United States is experiencing an
unprecedented   prosperous period. Homeownership hit a
record high level last   year. Unemployment is at its lowest
rate in almost 30 years.   Rapid technological innovation
has increased productivity and   created longer-sustainable
economic growth. Demand has   grown in all sectors.

However, some of America's citizens are being left behind.
Our nation is experiencing a crisis in affordable
multifamily   rental housing inventory. Ironically, rising
real estate markets   often translate into an increased
potential for the loss of   affordable housing rental
opportunities.

Rental housing opportunities are also shrinking because
the   subsidies and contracts on much of this nation's
regulated   housing supply are about to expire: Consider
the following:

Many owners of HUD-assisted affordable housing are
actively   choosing to exit government-sponsored
programs, whether   they are motivated by personal
lifestyle choice, HUD's   increased scrutiny of their
actions, or tax considerations.   According to data gathered
by the National Housing Trust,   private owners have
already "taken to market" over 100,000   HUD-assisted or

insured apartments, and 2,000 more such apartments are losing affordability monthly. The average rent hike associated with conversion from "regulated affordable" to market rate is 45 percent.

According to HUD, some 1.5 million privately owned, federally insured apartments using Section 8 will have their government contracts expire over the next five years alone. The unpaid principal balance on the loans on these properties is well over $50 billion!

Other potential affordable housing with expiring subsidies include housing subsidized by the Rural Housing Service and Low Income Housing Tax Credits.

The struggle for affordable housing is geographically widespread and includes the working poor. According to Harvard's Joint Center on Housing Studies, in no housing market in the nation --not Baltimore, not Iowa, not Texas, nowhere --can a household earning today's minimum wage reasonably afford a modest two-bedroom rental.| While the rest of our nation is well sheltered, the poor and very poor are living in overcrowded or dilapidated housing, or are spending a very large percentage of their discretionary income on shelter, placing rent in competition with other essentials, like food.

In short, structural changes that affect the availability of affordable housing are affecting the lives of those who need it profoundly. Perhaps the National Low Income Housing Coalition gave the most vivid picture of the life these lowincome families lead: "Like a high stakes game of musical chairs, the number of poor renters remains the same and they must compete for a diminishing number of affordable places to live."| Nonprofit Housing Acquisition: an Opportunity Emerges Within the potential loss of affordable housing lies an opportunity for nonprofit, mission-driven ownership. Toward this end, the National Housing Trust and the Enterprise Foundation have created the NHT/Enterprise Preservation Corporation ("NHT/Enterprise"), a 50l(c)(3) acquisition entity with the sole purpose of preserving affordable multifamily housing that serves very-low-income households. Initially, NHT/Enterprise will focus on government-subsidized apartments. We welcome opportunities to handle a portfolio, especially when no local organization has the capacity to work on a large scale. NHT/Enterprise also plans to purchase tax credit supported homes and unsubsidized apartments

NHT/Enterprise is unique in several ways:

The National Housing Trust and Enterprise have provided $1.3 million seed capital to the effort. An additional $1.7 million has been invested by the MacArthur Foundation, Fannie Mae Foundation and Freddie Mac.

NHT/Enterprise builds on the Trust and Enterprise's experience in acquisition and rehabilitation. The Trust has helped preserve more than 5,000 govemment-assisted apartments during the past six years. Enterprise Social Investment Corporation (ESIC) has raised more than $2.5 billion in equity from more than 180 different financial institutions to help create approximately 6,000 homes.
The response to NHT/Enterprise has been overwhelming. Owners of more than 40 properties in nine states have

already asked our organization to consider purchasing their properties, which average 80+ units with an unpaid principal balance of approximately $15,000 per apartment and rehabilitation costs of less than $5,000 per unit.

The Financial Services Role

Lenders can play a crucial role in this process. The new banking modernization laws permit banks and investment bankers to work under one roof. The efficiencies gained could be used to support nonprofit purchases of existing, multifamily housing. Mortgage lenders and investment bankers who now work for the same financial services company can help us achieve our social and economic goals. Consider the following products:

Bridge Financing: NHT/Enterprise and other nonprofits often want to tie down properties through a credit facility. This facility, typically six months to three years in duration, can be paid at market interest rate. The default "take-out" strategy for this type of financing is through a 501(c)(3) tax exempt bond. For example, NHT/Enterprise Preservation Corporation recently purchased a very-well-maintained 208-unit community located in Kissimmee, Florida. There, the bridge financing of approximately $8 million, provided by Bank of America at below prime, will be taken out by a Standard and Poor's or Moody's senior/subordinate bond debt structure.

Affirmative Action!

Affirmative action works. There are thousands of examples of situations where people of color, white women, and working class women and men of all races who were previously excluded from jobs or educational opportunities, or were denied opportunities once admitted, have gained access through affirmative action. When these policies received executive branch and judicial support, vast numbers of people of color, white women and men have gained access they would not otherwise have had. These gains have led to very real changes. Affirmative action programs have not eliminated racism, nor have they always been implemented without problems. However, there would be no struggle to roll back the gains achieved if affirmative action policies were ineffective.

Debates about affirmative action are about more than legal issues. Taking action to end racism is the challenge and responsibility of every single person in our society, as well as of the institutions and organizations which have such a large impact on our lives. Yet today there is a vocal minority who   want to stop affirmative action not only as a legal remedy, but   also as a social commitment. Now that affirmative action has   led to some social changes there are those who are saying our   society has gone too far in correcting racial injustice. Of   course, this vocal minority is not challenging traditional forms   of preference and discrimination that favor the rich, the educated, white people and men.

Affirmative action is practiced in many areas of our society in   addition to leveling the playing field for people of color. There   are hiring and recruiting preferences for veterans, women, the   children of alumni of many universities. There are special   economic incentives for purchase of U.S.-made products,   import quotas against foreign goods, and agricultural and   textile subsidies. Over many decades these practices have led   to a huge over-representation of white people, men and people   of middle, upper middle and upper class backgrounds in our universities, in well-paid jobs, and in the professions. One indication that attacks on affirmative action are part of a white   backlash against equality is that affirmative action in the form   of preferences that primarily benefit white people are not   being questioned.

Affirmative action measures were established to fight racial   discrimination. The federal government mandated affirmative   action programs to redress racial inequality and injustice in a   series of steps beginning with an executive order issued by   President Kennedy in 1961. The Civil Rights Act of 1964   made discrimination illegal and established equal employment   opportunity for all Americans regardless of race, cultural   background, color or religion. Subsequent executive orders, in   particular

Executive Order 11246 issued by President Johnson in September 1965, mandated affirmative action goals for all federally funded programs and moved monitoring and enforcement of affirmative action programs out of the White House and into the Labor Department. These policies and the government action that followed were a response to the tremendous mobilization of African Americans and white supporters during the late 1950s and early 1960s pushing for integration and racial Justice.

Initially, affirmative action was a policy primarily aimed at correcting institutional discrimination where decisions, policies and procedures that are not necessarily explicitly discriminatory have had a negative impact on people of color. Affirmative action policies address and redress systematic economic and political discrimination against any group of people that are underrepresented or have a history of being discriminated against in particular institutions. Beneficiaries of these programs have included white men and women, people with disabilities, and poor and working class people, but their primary emphasis has been on addressing racial discrimination.

There is pervasive racism in all areas of U.S. society. For example, in 1991 Diane Sawyer with ABC- TV filmed two men, one African American and one white, who were matched for age, appearance, education, and other qualities. They were followed for a day by a camera crew. The white man received service in stores while the African American was ignored, or in some cases, watched closely. The white man was offered a lower price and better financing at a car dealership. There were jobs where the African American was turned down, and apartments for rent after the African American man was told   they were no longer available. A police car passed the white   man while he was walking down the street but it slowed down   and took note of the African American.(1) Hundreds of studies   demonstrate discrimination against people of color in different   areas of everyday life.

Racism, rather than being self-correcting, is self perpetuating.   The disadvantages to people of color and the benefits to white   people are passed on to each succeeding generation unless   remedial action is taken. The disadvantages to people of color   coalesce into institutional practices which, although they may   be race neutral in intent, adversely affect people of color. It has proven necessary to take positive steps to eliminate and compensate for these institutional effects of racism, even when there is no discernible discriminatory intent.
For example, most job opportunities are heard about through   informal networks of friends, family and neighbors. Since the   results of racism are segregated communities, schools and   workplaces, this pattern leaves people of color out of the loop   for many jobs, advancement opportunities, scholarships and   training programs. Federal law now requires widespread and public advertisement of such opportunities so that not only people of color, but white women and men who are outside   the circles of information, have an equal opportunity to apply for these positions.

Another area affirmative action addresses is preferential hiring   programs. Many times people of color have been excluded   from hiring pools, overtly discriminated against, unfairly   eliminated because of inappropriate qualification standards, or   have been rendered unqualified because of discrimination in   education and housing. Court decisions on affirmative action   have rendered illegal those qualifications that are not relevant to one's ability to do the job. They have also mandated hiring   goals so that those employed begin to reflect the racial mix of   the general population from which workers are drawn. There   is no legal requirement to ever hire an unqualified person.   There is a mandate that in choosing between qualified   candidates, the hiring preference should be for a person of   color when past discrimination has resulted in white people

receiving preferential treatment.

Sometimes people argue that affirmative action means the best   qualified person will not be hired. However, it has been   demonstrated many times in hiring and academic recruitment   that test and educational qualifications are not necessarily the   best predictors of future success. This does not mean   unqualified people should be hired. It means basically   qualified people who may not have the highest test scores or   grades, but who are eminently ready to do the job may be   hired. Employers have traditionally hired people not only on   test scores, but on personal appearance, family and personal   connections, school ties and on race and gender preferences,   demonstrating that talent or desirability can be defined in many   ways. These practices have all contributed to a segregated   work force where whites hold the best jobs, and people of   color work in the least desirable and most poorly paid   positions. Affirmative action policies serve as a corrective to   such patterns of discrimination. They keep score on progress toward proportional representation and place the burden of proof on organizations to show why it is not possible to achieve it.

It has been argued that affirmative action benefits people of color who are already well off or have middle class advantages, not the poor and working class people of color who most need it. A more careful analysis reveals that affirmative action programs have benefited substantial numbers of poor and working class people of color. Access to job training programs, vocational schools, and semi-skilled and skilled blue-collar, craft, pink-collar, police and firefighter jobs has increased substantially through affirmative action programs. Even in the professions, many people of color who have benefited from affirmative action have been from

families of low income and job status. (2)

Middle class people of color have also benefited from affirmative action. All people of color have experienced the effects of racial discrimination. Having more money may buffer the most extreme effects, but it doesn't protect people from everyday racial discrimination. The middle class in various communities of color is small and often fragile. Its members own less wealth and have less financial security than their white counterparts because of the past effects of racial discrimination. They also experience the full range of cultural racism and white prejudice that all people of color have to deal with.

Another argument raised against affirmative action is that individual white people, often white males, have to pay for past discrimination and may not get the jobs they deserve. It is true that specific white people may not get specific job opportunities because of affirmative action policies and may   suffer as a result. This lack of opportunity is unfortunate; the   structural factors which produce a lack of decent jobs needs to   be addressed. It must not be forgotten that millions of specific   people of color have also lost specific job opportunities as a   result of racial discrimination. To be concerned only with the   white applicants who don't get the job, and not with the people of color who don't, is showing racial preference.

But how true is it that white male candidates are being discriminated against or are losing out because of affirmative   action programs? If one looks at the composition of various   professions such as law, medicine, architecture, academics and   journalism, or at corporate management, or at higher-level   government positionsor if one looks overall at the average   income levels of white menone immediately notices that   people of color are still significantly underrepresented and underpaid in every category. People of color don't make up the   proportions of these jobs even remotely equal to their percentage of the population. They don't earn wages comparable to white men. White men are tremendously overrepresented in almost any category of work that is highly   rewarded except for professional athletics. According to a   1995 government report, white males make up only 29   percent of the workforce, but they hold 95 percent of senior   management positions. (3) Until there is both equal   opportunity and fair distribution of education, training and   advancement to all Americans, affirmative action for people of   color will be necessary to counter the hundreds of years of   affirmative action that has been directed at white males. It   cannot reasonably be argued that white males are   discriminated against as a group if they are over-represented in   most high status categories.

Two other aspects of this dynamic should be noted. Although all white people benefit from racism, white men receive more of the economic and other benefits of racism than white women of the same socio-economic status. White men have always been favored in families and schools and preferred for jobs, training, educational programs, athletic programs, military careers and job advancement and promotion. Men still make more than women for comparable work, are given better educational opportunities, have more leisure time and are accorded higher status than women.

The second and equally important part of this dynamic is that not all white men are equal. If you are a white male you may or may not have gained a lot from racism. If you are not welloff, well educated or well rewarded in your life, you should look at white men who are and analyze how they accumulated such rewards. Why do many corporate executives make more in a week than their workers make in a year? Why does the average CEO "earn" as much as 157 factory workers?(4) Business leaders are able to exploit male workers by appealing to common bonds and common fears among white men. They have played on white male fears of losing their jobs (and their manliness) to keep them working hard, claiming that only white men had the strength, skill, intelligence, independence, strength of character and virility to do the job. White workers have often bought these arguments feeling pride and increased self-esteem in their working abilities, and feeling personally threatened by the presence of people of color and white women in the workplace. Their ability to fight against low wages, unsafe working conditions, the restructuring of their jobs and plant closures has been diminished even while they thought they were protecting their jobs through race riots, anti-immigration laws, attacks on affirmative action and workplace discrimination, harassment and exclusion. Collusion with well-off white men against affirmative action is not in the best interests of poor, working and middle class men. Yet many have bought the lie that who they are is based on the manliness of the work they do and their ability to keep their workplaces as white male preserves.(5) Affirmative action helps mitigate the historical effects of institutional racism. It also counters the effects of current discrimination, intentional or not. Not all white people are well intentioned. Some believe that everyone should have an equal chance but still hold deep seated prejudices against people of color. For a substantial number of whites, however well- intentioned, those prejudices lead to discrimination. Without specific, numerical goals, it has been found that many people and organizations continue to practice discrimination while professing agreement with equal opportunity. There are so many subtle and not-so-subtle ways to eliminate people of color from the job application process it is not surprising that employers have found ways around affirmative action unless it is tied to visible hiring and promotion targets. In a society with such overwhelming evidence of racism, it must be assumed that individuals and organizations will resist efforts to end it. For instance, in 1993 the Equal Employment Opportunity Commission had a backlog of 70,000 discrimination cases.(6) It is necessary to set goals and enforce and monitor standards because this is the only way compliance can be measured. These are the mechanisms needed to ensure that affirmative action is more than a facade. These mechanisms are not quotas. Quotas have been used in the past to exclude particular groups of people from jobs or educational opportunities. They have been used to limit the number of Asian Americans or Jews in universities so white people would continue to have unequal access. Setting minimum goals for inclusion is the opposite of setting maximums. We need numerical goals to guarantee compliance with affirmative action policies. Numerical goals promote democratic access to education, jobs and job training. Some people have claimed that affirmative action programs lower self-esteem in those who are favored by them, perhaps even in those individuals who do not directly benefit from them. There is no systematic evidence for this effect. It seems to be something that white people worry about more than people of color. Persistent denial of equal opportunityand therefore inadequate access to good jobs, good education and housing leads to poor self-esteem. It is discrimination that seems to be the more important harm to eliminate. People who are truly worried about low self-esteem among people of color should be strong advocates for effective affirmative action programs to counter discrimination.

Affirmative action programs have been effective in many areas of public life because they opened up opportunities for people who would not otherwise have them, including white women and men. Attacks on affirmative action are part of a systematic attempt to roll back progress in ending discrimination and to curtail a broad social commitment to justice and equality. Attacking affirmative action is self-destructive for all of us except the rich.

Affirmative action is not a cure-all. It will not eliminate racial discrimination, nor will it eliminate competition for scarce resources. Affirmative action programs can only ensure that everyone has a fair chance at what is available. They cannot direct us to the social policies necessary so people do not have to compete for scarce resources in the first place. The larger question to ask is why are there not enough decent paying, challenging and safe jobs for everyone? Why are there not enough seats in the universities for everyone who wants an education? Expanding opportunity for people of color means expanding not only their access to existing jobs, education and housing (affirmative action), but also removing the obstacles that cause these resources to be limited (social justice).

Affirmative action has been a symbol of white people's acknowledgment of and serious concerns to eradicating racial discrimination. It has been interpreted as such by most people of color. It is crucial that at this stage of backlash against the gains of the last three decades, we do not abandon programs

that counter the effects of discrimination.

When whites attack affirmative action if they are truly committed to American ideals of justice and equalitythey should be proposing other remedies for racial inequality in our society. The hypocrisy is clear when white people who say they support equal opportunity attack affirmative action, yet want to leave intact the basic economic and racial injustices it is designed to correct. Ask people who oppose affirmative action how they propose to eliminate racial discrimination. You can learn a lot about their true beliefs from their answers.

The California Evans Civil Rights Act will restore
Affirmative Action to Higher Education and make
Public Colleges Free.

Affirmative Action   Alive & Well

For more than two decades, affirmative action has been under   sustained assault. In courts, legislatures, and the media,   opponents have condemned it as an unprincipled program of   racial and gender preferences that threatens fundamental   American values of fairness, equality, and democratic   opportunity. Such preferences, they say, are extraordinary departures from prevailing "meritocratic" modes of selection,   which they present as both fair and functional: fair, because   they treat all candidates as equals; functional, because they are   well suited to picking the best candidates.

This challenge to affirmative action has met with concerted   response. Defenders argue that affirmative action is still   needed to rectify continued exclusion and marginalization.   And they marshal considerable evidence showing that   conventional standards of selection exclude women and   people of color, and that people who were excluded in the past   do not yet operate on a level playing field. But this response   has largely been reactive. Proponents typically treat   affirmative action as a crucial but peripheral supplement to an   essentially sound framework of selection for jobs and schools.

We think it is time to shift the terrain of debate. We need to   situate the conversation about race, gender, and affirmative   action in a wider account of democratic opportunity by   refocusing attention from the contested periphery of the   system of selection to its settled core. The present system   measures merit through scores on paper-and-pencil tests. But this measure is fundamentally unfair. In the educational setting, it restricts opportunities for many poor and working class Americans of all colors and genders who could otherwise obtain a better education. In the employment setting, it restricts access based on inadequate predictors of job performance. In short, it is neither fair nor functional in its distribution of opportunities for admission to higher education, entry-level hiring, and job promotion.

To be sure, the exclusion experienced by women and people of color is especially revealing of larger patterns. The race- and gender-based exclusions that are the target of current affirmative action policies remain the most visible examples of bias in ostensibly neutral selection processes. Objectionable in themselves, these exclusions also signal the inadequacy of traditional methods of selection for everyone, and the need to rethink how we allocate educational and employment opportunities. And that rethinking is crucial to our capacity to develop productive, fair, and efficient institutions that can meet the challenges of a rapidly changing and increasingly complex marketplace. By using the experience of those on the margin to rethink the whole, we may forge a new, progressive vision of cross-racial collaboration, functional diversity, and genuinely democratic opportunity.

Affirmative Action Narratives

Competing narratives drive the affirmative action debate. The stock story told by critics in the context of employment concerns the white civil servant-say a police officer or firefighter-John Doe. (Similar stories abound in the educational setting.) Doe scores several points higher on the civil service exam and interview rating process, but loses out to a woman or person of color who did not score as high on those selection criteria.1

Doe and others in similar circumstances advance two basic claims: first, that they have more merit than beneficiaries of affirmative action; and second, that as a matter of fairness they are entitled to the position for which they applied. Consider these claims in turn.

The idea of merit can be interpreted in a variety of ways: for example, as a matter of desert (because they were next in line, based on established criteria of selection, they deserve the position), or as earned recognition ("when an individual has worked hard and succeeded, she deserves recognition, praise and/or reward"2). But, most fundamentally, arguments about merit are functional: a person merits a job if he or she has, to an especially high degree, the qualities needed to perform well in that job. Many critics of affirmative action equate merit, functionally understood, with a numerical ranking on standard paper-and-pencil tests. Those with higher scores are presumed to be most qualified, and therefore most deserving.

Fairness, like merit, is a concept with varying definitions. The stock story defines fairness formally. Fairness, it assumes, requires treating everyone the same: allowing everyone to enter the competition for a position, and evaluating each personÆs results the same way. If everyone takes the same test, and every applicantÆs test is evaluated in the same manner, then the assessment is fair. So affirmative action is unfair because it takes race and gender into account, and thus evaluates some test results differently. A crucial premise of this fairness challenge to affirmative action is the assumption that tests afford equal opportunity to demonstrate individual merit, and therefore are not biased.

Underlying the standard claims about merit and fairness, then, is the idea that we have an objective yardstick for measuring qualification. Institutions are assumed to know what they are looking for (to continue the yardstick analogy, length), how to measure it (yards, meters), how to replicate the measurement process (using the ruler), and how to rank people accordingly (by height). Both critics and proponents of affirmative action typically assume that objective tests for particular attributes of merit-perhaps supplemented by subjective methods such as unstructured interviews and reference checks-can be justified as predictive of performance, and as the most efficient method of selection.

Merit, Fairness, and Testocracy

The basic premise of the stock narrative is that the selection criteria and processes used to rank applicants for jobs and admission to schools are fair and valid tests of merit. This premise is flawed. The conventional system of selection does not give everyone an equal opportunity to compete. Not everyone who could do the job, or could bring new insights about how to do the job even better, is given an opportunity to perform or succeed. The yardstick metaphor simply does not withstand scrutiny.

Fictive Merit

For present purposes, we accept the idea that capacity to perform-functional merit-is a legitimate consideration in distributing jobs and educational opportunities. But we dispute the notion that merit is identical to performance on standardized tests. Such tests do not fulfill their stated function. They do not reliably identify those applicants who will succeed in college or later in life, nor do they consistently predict those who are most likely to perform well in the jobs they will occupy. Particularly when used alone or to rankorder candidates, timed paper-and-pencil tests screen out applicants who could nevertheless do the job.

Those who use standardized tests need to be able to identify and measure successful performance in the job or at school. In both contexts, however, those who use tests lack meaningful measures of successful performance. In the employment area, many employers have not attempted to correlate test performance with worker productivity or pay. In the educational context, researchers have attempted to correlate

standardized tests with first-year performance in college or post-graduate education.

But this measure does not reflect successful overall academic achievement or performance in other areas valued by the educational institution. Moreover, "successful performance" needs to be interpreted broadly. A study of three classes of Harvard alumni over three decades, for example, found a high correlation between "success"-defined by income, community involvement, and professional satisfaction-and two criteria that might not ordinarily be associated with Harvard freshmen: low SAT scores and a blue-collar background.

When asked what predicts life success, college admissions officers at elite universities report that, above a minimum level of competence, "initiative" or "drive" are the best predictors.

By contrast, the conventional measures attempt to predict successful performance, narrowly defined, in the short-run. They focus on immediate success in school and a short timeframe between taking the test and demonstrating success. Those who excel based on those short-term measures, however, may not in fact excel over the long-run in areas that are equally or more important. For example, a study of graduates of the University of Michigan Law School found a negative relationship between high LSAT scores and subsequent community leadership or community service.

Those with higher LSAT scores are less likely, as a general matter, to serve their community or do pro bono service as a lawyer. In addition, the study found that admission indexesincluding the LSAT-fail to correlate with other accomplishments after law school, including income levels

and career satisfaction.

Standardized tests may thus compromise an institution's capacity to search for what it really values in selection. Privileging the aspects of performance measured by standardized tests may well screen out the contributions of people who would bring important and different skills to the workplace or educational institution. It may reward passive learning styles that mimic established strategies rather than creative, critical, or innovative thinking.

Finally, individuals often perform better in both workplace and school when challenged by competing perspectives or when given the opportunity to develop in conjunction with the different approaches or skills of others.

The problem of using standardized tests to predict performance is particularly acute in the context of employment. Standardized tests may reward qualities such as willingness to guess, conformity, and docility. If they do, then test performance may not relate significantly to the capacity to function well in jobs that require creativity, judgment, and leadership. In a service economy, creativity and interpersonal skills are important, though hard to measure. In the stock scenario of civil service exams for police and fire departments, traits such as honesty, perseverance, courage, and ability to manage anger are left out. In other words, people who rely heavily on numbers to make employment decisions may be looking in the wrong place. While John Doe scored higher on the civil service exam, he may not perform better as a police officer.

Fictive Fairness

Scores on standardized tests are, then, inadequate measures of merit. But are the conventional methods of selecting candidates for high-stakes positions fair? The stock affirmative action narrative implicitly embraces the idea that fairness consists in sameness of treatment. But this conception of fairness assumes a level playing field-that if everyone plays by the same rules, the game does not favor or disadvantage anyone.

An alternative conception of fairness-we call it "fairness as equal access and opportunity"-rejects the automatic equation of sameness with fairness. It focuses on providing members of various races and genders with opportunities to demonstrate their capacities and recognizes that formal sameness can camouflage actual difference and apparently neutral screening devices can be exclusionary. The central idea is that the standards governing the process must not arbitrarily advantage members of one group over another. It is not "fair," in this sense, to use entry-level credentials that appear to treat everyone the same, but in effect deny women and people of color a genuine opportunity to demonstrate their capacities.

On this conception, the "testocracy" fails to provide a fair playing field for candidates. Many standardized tests assume   that there is a single way to complete a job, and assess   applicants solely on the basis of this uniform style. In this way,   the testing process arbitrarily excludes individuals who may   perform equally effectively, but with different approaches.

For example, in many police departments, strength, military   experience, and speed weigh heavily in the decision to hire   police officers. These characteristics relate to a particular   mode of policing focusing on "command presence" and   control through authority and force.7

If the job of policing is defined as subduing dangerous suspects, then it makes sense to favor the strongest, fastest, and most disciplined candidates. But not every situation calls   for quick reaction time. Indeed, in some situations, responding   quickly gets police officers and whole departments in trouble.

This speed-and-strength standard normalizes a particular type   of officer: tough, brawny, and macho. But other modes of   policing-dispute resolution, persuasion, counseling, and   community involvement-are also critical, and sometimes   superior, approaches to policing. One study of the Los Angeles   Police Department, conducted in the wake of the Rodney King   trials, recommended that the department increase the number   of women on the police force as part of a strategy to reduce   police brutality and improve community relations. The study found that women often display a more interactive and engaged approach to policing.8

Similarly, an informal survey of police work in some New

York City Housing Authority projects found that many women housing authority officers, because they could not rely on their brawn to intimidate potential offenders, developed a mentoring style with young adolescent males.9 The women, many of whom came from the community they were patrolling, increased public safety because they did not approach the young men in a confrontational way. Their authority was respected because they offered respect. The retention and success of new entrants to institutions often depend on expanding measures of successful performance. But because conventional measures camouflage their bias, one-size-fits-all testocracies invite people to believe that they have earned their status because of a test score, and invite beneficiaries of affirmative action to believe exactly the opposite-that they did not earn their opportunity. By allowing partial and underinclusive selection standards to proceed without criticism, affirmative action perpetuates an asymmetrical approach to evaluation.

In addition to arbitrarily favoring certain standards of performance, conventional selection methods advantage candidates from higher socioeconomic backgrounds and disproportionately screen out women and people of color, as well as those in lower income brackets. When combined with other unstructured screening practices, such as personal connections and alumni preferences, standardized testing creates an arbitrary barrier for many otherwise-qualified candidates.

The evidence that the testocracy is skewed in favor of wealthy contestants is consistent and striking. Consider the linkage between test performance and parental income. Average family income rises with each 100-point increase in SAT scores, except for the highest SAT category, where the number of cases is small. Within each racial and ethnic group, SAT scores increase with income.

Reliance on high school rank alone excludes fewer people from lower socioeconomic backgrounds. When the SAT is used in conjunction with high school rank to select college applicants, the number of applicants admitted from lowerincome families decreases. This is because the SAT is more strongly correlated with every measure of socioeconomic background than is high school rank.

Existing methods of selection, both objective and subjective, also exclude people based on their race and gender. For example, although women as a group perform worse than males on the SAT, they equal or outperform men in grade point average during the first year of college, the most common measure of successful performance. Similar patterns have been detected in the results of the ACT and other standardized college selection tests.

Supplementing class rank with the SAT also decreases black acceptances and black enrollments. Studies show that the group of black applicants rejected based on their SAT scores includes both those who would likely have failed and those who would likely have succeeded, and that these groups offset each other. Consequently, the rejection of more blacks as a result of using SAT scores "does not translate into improved admissions outcomes. The SAT does not improve colleges' ability to admit successful blacks and reject potentially unsuccessful ones."

Thus, it is incontestable that the existing meritocracy disproportionately includes wealthy white men. Is this highly unequal outcome fair? Even if the "meritocracy" screens out women, people of color, and those of lower socioeconomic status, it could be argued that those screens are fair if they serve an important function. But the testocracy fails even on this measure; it does not reliably distinguish successful future performers from unsuccessful ones, even when supplemented by additional subjective criteria. Therefore, racial, gender, and socioeconomic exclusion cannot legitimately be justified in the name of a flawed system of selection.

A New Approach

We have seen how the stock affirmative action narrative normalizes and legitimates selection practices that are neither functional nor fair. Now it is time to use these criticisms as an occasion to move from affirmative action as an add-on to affirmative action as an occasion to rethink the organizing framework for selection generally.

Such rethinking should begin by reconsidering the connection between predetermined qualifications and future performance. The standard approach proceeds as if selection were a finetuned matching process that measures the capacity to perform according to some predetermined criteria of performance. This assumes that the capacity to perform-functional merit-exists in people apart from their opportunity to work on the job. It further assumes that institutions know in advance what they are looking for, and that these functions will remain constant across a wide range of work sites and over time.

But neither candidates nor positions remain fixed. Often people who have been given an opportunity to do a job perform well because they learn the job by doing it. Moreover, on-the-job learning has assumed even greater significance in the current economy, in which unstable markets, technological advances, and shorter product cycles have created pressures for businesses to increase the flexibility and problem-solving capacity of workers. Under these circumstances, access to onthe-job training opportunities will contribute to functional merit-the opportunity to perform will precede the capacity.

The concept of selection as a matching process also presumes that institutions have a clear idea of what they value, and of the relationship of particular jobs to their institutional goals. Even in a relatively stable economic and technological environment, institutions rarely attempt to articulate goals, much less develop a basis for measuring successful achievement of those goals. But without a definition of successful performance, it is difficult to develop fair and valid selection criteria and processes.

Defining successful performance has also become more complicated in the current economic and political environment. Traditional measures of success, such as shortterm profitability, do not fully define success, and may in fact distort the capacity to evaluate and monitor employee performance. In addition, standards must increasingly change to adapt to technological developments and shifting consumer demand. Students of economic organization and human resources now emphasize the importance of developing complex, interactive, and holistic approaches to measuring both institutional and individual performance.14 Conventional matching approaches to selection do not easily accommodate this move toward more dynamic and interrelated assessments of successful performance.

Current selection approaches also focus on the select gifted   individual, who is assumed to possess merit in the abstract and   to demonstrate it through a test or interview. Social science   evidence shows that the testing environment can selectively   depress the test performance of highly qualified individuals. And individual performance does not take into account how   an applicant functions as part of a group. Increasingly, work   requires the capacity to interact effectively with others, and the demands of the economy are moving in the direction of more   interactive, team-oriented production. The capacity to adapt to   rapid changes in technology, shifts in consumer preferences,   and fluid markets for goods requires greater collaboration at   every level.16 Paper-and-pencil tests do not measure or   predict an individual's capacity for creativity and   collaboration.

Assessment through opportunity to perform often works better   than testing for performance. Various studies have shown that   "experts often fail on formal measures of their calculating or   reasoning capacities but can be shown to exhibit precisely   those same skills in the course of their ordinary work."17   Those who assess individuals in situations that more closely   resemble actual working conditions make better predictions   about those individual's ultimate performance. Particularly   when those assessments are integrated into day-to-day work over a period of time, they have the potential to produce better   information about workers and better workers.

Moreover, many of those who are given an opportunity to perform, even when their basic preparation is weaker, catch up   if they are motivated to achieve. Indeed, a recent study of a 25year policy of open admissions at the City University of New   York found that the school was one of the largest sources in   the United States of undergraduate students going on to earn   doctorates, even though many of its undergraduates come   from relatively poor backgrounds and take twice as long to   complete their bachelors degree.18

Reclaiming Merit and Fairness

Critics of affirmative action defend prevailing selection practices in the name of meritocracy and democracy. We have argued that those practices put democratic opportunity fundamentally at risk. Even when they are modified by a commitment to affirmative action, current modes of selection jeopardize democratic values of inclusiveness (no one is arbitrarily shut out or excluded); transparency (the processes employed are open and are functionally linked to the public character or public mission of the institution); and accountability (the choice of beneficiaries is directly linked to a public good).

The failure of existing practice to achieve inclusiveness is perhaps the most telling. Although some people will lose as a result of any sorting and ranking, a democratic system needs to give those losers a sense of hope in the future, not divide us into classes of permanent losers and permanent winners. But that is precisely what happens when we make opportunity dependent on past success.

How, then, can we develop a model of selection that expresses a more inclusive, transparent, and accountable vision of democratic opportunity-an approach to selection that will benefit everyone, and advance racial and gender justice?

An Emerging Model

Because of the importance in a democracy of ensuring opportunities to perform, we can start by shifting the model of selection from prediction to performance. This model builds on the insight that the opportunity to participate helps to create the capacity to perform, and that actual performance offers the best evidence of capacity to perform. So instead of making opportunity depend on a strong prior showing of qualification, we should expand opportunities as a way of building the relevant qualifications.

To follow this model, organizations need to build assessment into their activities, integrate considerations of inclusion and diversity into the process of selection, and develop mechanisms of evaluation that are accountable to those considerations. The result would be a dynamic process of selection, with feedback integrated into productivity. At the level of individual performance assessment, it would mean less reliance on one-shot predictive tests and more on performance-based evaluation.

One fundamental change resulting from our framework would be a shift away from reliance on tests as a means of distinguishing among candidates. Tests would be limited to screening out individuals who could not learn to perform competently with adequate training and mentoring, or be simply discontinued as a part of the selection process. Of course, decreasing reliance on tests to rank candidates would create the need to develop other ways of distinguishing among applicants. There is no single, uniform solution to this problem. One approach would be a lottery system that would distribute opportunity to participate among relatively indistinguishable candidates by chance. Concerns about a lottery insensitivity to particular institutional needs or values could be addressed by increasing the selection prospects of applicants with skills, abilities, or backgrounds that are particularly valued by the institution. A weighted lottery may be the fairest and most functional approach for some institutions. Particularly in the education arena, where opportunity lies at the core of the institutions mission, a lottery may be an important advance. Above that testdetermined floor, applicants could be chosen by several alternatives, including portfolio-based assessment or a more structured and participatory decision-making process. A more institutionally grounded approach might work in non-educational contexts. In some jobs, for example, decision-makers would assume responsibility for constructing a dynamic and interactive process of selection that is integrated into the day-to-day functioning of the organization. Recent developments in the assessment area, such as portfolio-based and authentic assessment, move in this direction. These might build on the tradition and virtues of apprenticeship, and indeed might "more closely resemble traditional apprenticeship measures than formal testing."20 They would build from and acknowledge the effects of context on performance and the importance of measuring performance in relation to context.

To take the next step in developing an experience-based approach to opportunity and assessment, it would be necessary   to consider the needs, interests, and possibilities of the   particular institutional setting. The central challenge is to   develop systems of accountable decision-making that   minimize the expression of bias, and structure judgment   around identified, although not static, norms. For each   assessment, decision-makers would articulate criteria of   successful performance, document activities and tasks relevant   to the judgment, assess candidates in relation to those criteria,   and offer sufficient information about the candidates performance to enable others to exercise independent   judgment.

For this model to work, institutions would also need to change the relationship between race, gender, and other categories of exclusion to the overall decision-making process. Institutions would continue to assess the impact of various selection processes on traditionally excluded groups.   But institutions would use that information in different ways.   Rather than operating as an add-on, after-the-fact response to   failures of the overall process, race and gender would serve as   both a signal of organizational failure and a catalyst of   organizational innovation. We will return to this issue later,   but let's first try to imagine what this more integrated   approach would look like.

Consider the case of Bernice, now the general counsel of a major financial institution. Initially, she was hired as local general counsel to a bank, after having previously been partner in a prestigious law firm. (She left the firm after reaching the glass ceiling, unable to bring in enough new clients to progress further.)

Bernice ultimately became general counsel to a major national corporation that previously had no women in high-level management positions. Her promotion resulted from the opportunities presented in an interactive and extended selection process. Her local bank merged with a larger company. In part to create the appearance of including women, she was permitted to compete for the job of general counsel for the new entity. Three lawyers shared the position for nine months. She initially did not view herself as in the running for the final cut.

During this time period, Bernice had a series of contacts with high-level corporate officials, contacts she never would have had without this probationary team approach. As it turned out, Bernice was able to deal unusually well with a series of crises.

If standard criteria, such as recommendations and interpersonal contacts, had been used to select a candidate, it is doubtful Bernice would have been picked. But teamwork, decentralized management, and collaborative and flexible working relationships allowed her to develop the contacts and experiences that trained her.

The opportunity to interact over a period of time allowed her to demonstrate her strengths to those who made promotion   decisions. Bernice did not know she had those strengths until

she took the job.

Now, as general counsel, she is positioned to expand opportunities for women, and corporate culture in general. She can structure the same kind of collaborative decision-making in selection that provided her the opportunity to work   her way into the job. She determines who is promoted within   the legal department, and who is hired as outside counsel. She   is also in a position to influence how women are assessed as   managers within the company.

This story illustrates the potential for integrating concerns about diversity into the process of recruitment and selection. It   also shows the value of using performance to assess   performance. At the core of this integrative move is a   functional theory of diversity animated both by principles of   justice and fairness (the inclusion of marginalized groups and   the minimization of bias) and by strategic concerns (improving   productivity). It is crucial to this integration that decisionmakers and advocates understand and embrace a conception of   diversity that comprises normative and instrumental elements.   In public discourse, diversity has become a catchall phrase   used to substitute for a variety of goals, or a numerical   concept that is equated with proportional representation.

Too often, the different strands of diversity remain separate,   with those concerned about justice emphasizing racial and   gender diversity as a project of remediation, and those   concerned about productivity emphasizing differences in   background and skills. Without an articulated theory that links   diversity to the goals of particular enterprises and to the   project of racial justice, public discussion and public policymaking around race and gender issues is more complicated.

Selection and Productivity

One argument for more closely integrating selection and performance is that doing so has the potential to improve institutions' capacity to select productive workers, pursue innovative performance, and adapt quickly to the demands of a changing economic environment. The conventional top-down approach short-circuits the capacity of selection to serve as a mechanism for feedback about an institution's performance and its need to adapt to changing conditions. It also keeps institutions from developing more responsive, integrated, and dynamically efficient selection processes.

Instead of relying on standardized tests, the system of performance based selection would focus decision-makers attention on creating suitable scenarios for making informed judgments about performance. This would improve the capacity of institutions to find people who are creative, adaptive, reliable, and committed, rather than just good testtakers. In some instances, these structured opportunities could directly contribute to the productivity of the organization.

A more interactive process of selection also provides an ongoing opportunity to assess and monitor organizational performance and to perceive and react to the changing character and needs of clients and employees. It provides information learned through the process of selection to the rest of the organization. In the process of redefining the standards for recruitment, the organization also redefines how those already in the institution should function. Selection operates at the boundaries of the organization. It exposes decision-makers to the environment they operate in, provides access to information about the world in which the organization operates, and forces choices about its relationship with that environment. The process of defining the standards for positions also reflects and re-inscribes the organizations priorities and direction. Emphasizing one set of skills over another in the selection process communicates to employees and students how the organization defines good work. Thus, the selection process provides the opportunity and challenge of continually redefining standards in relation to stakeholders, both inside and outside of the organization.

The Benefits of Diversity

More open-ended processes of selection also embrace and harness difference. And the resulting diversity-in particular, an interactive dynamic among individuals with different vantage points, skills, or values-appears to help generate creative solutions to problems.

Studies have shown that work-team heterogeneity promotes more critical strategic analysis, creativity, innovation, and high-quality decisions. Analyses of group decision-making suggest that participation of groups with different prior beliefs or predispositions in decision making improves the quality of the decision for everyone. Studies of jury deliberations support the contention that diversity of participants contributes to improved deliberation. A jury consisting of people from diverse backgrounds has more accurate recall and a better understanding of the behavior of the parties than [a more homogeneous jury]."

Diversity in culture, style, and background also enhances the knowledge base and repertoire of skills and responses available to a particular group or institution, which can enhance institutions' capacity to perform and innovate. Again, the example of the Los Angeles Police Department illustrates this theory. The benefits of racial and gender diversity may be most obvious in the educational and human services areas, where customers, clients, and perspectives may themselves be identified by race and gender.

Racial and cultural diversity in a workforce can also provide   opportunities for companies marketing products that serve   racially and culturally diverse client groups. As David Thomas   and Robin Ely have documented, customers and clients from   different racial, ethnic, and cultural communities constitute   distinctive market niches that companies have sought to   address by diversifying their workforces.

Inside an organization, the experience of those who have been   excluded or marginalized often signals more general or   systemic problems that affect a much larger group and may   hurt the organization's overall productivity. Race and gender   complaints may be symptomatic of more general management   problems, such as poor organization or arbitrary treatment of   workers. For example, recent studies documenting that many   women find law school silencing and exclusionary reveal   patterns of problems that many men experience as well.

Similarly, sexual harassment of graduate students sometimes   reveals a more general institutional inadequacy that would   otherwise remain hidden. Faculty and students frequently lack   shared understandings about fair, respectful, non-exploitative   supervisory relationships between students and their faculty   advisors. Addressing sexual harassment-a problem ordinarily associated with women-can prompt a conversation on ways to   promote productive and successful working relationships in   general.

These observations answer a large question about the status of affirmative action in the performance-based model: Once we use the lens of the margins to rethink the whole, why do group status and performance continue to be crucial in assessing the adequacy of selection criteria? If we are successful in transforming the discourse and practice of merit and selection for everyone, why are race, gender, and other categories of exclusion still relevant to the discussion?

In responding to this question, we take the world as it currently exists. The workforce is becoming increasingly diverse: almost two-thirds of entrants to the civilian workforce in the period between 1992 and 2005 are projected to be women and racial minorities. Women and people of color have long been excluded and marginalized, and continue to experience exclusion in many institutional settings. Race continues to be a divisive issue for many Americans, one that prompts skepticism and mistrust. Our continued focus on race and gender moves forward from the current legal and organizational landscape. In many institutions, particularly those that are private and non-union, categories such as race and gender offer the only avenue for challenging decisions and practices.

Under these conditions, race- and gender-based inquiries continue to form the cornerstone of an integrated approach to a progressive economic agenda. Many members of marginalized groups predicate their willingness to participate in collaborative conversation on the majority's recognition of the ongoing significance of group-based exclusion. For members of historically excluded groups, a meaningful program of inclusion is a prerequisite to participating in ventures that benefit the whole community. Affirmative action has become a symbol of society's recognition of its responsibility for its history of legal disenfranchisement, and of the equal citizenship and respect of those who have historically been excluded. History shapes the perception and experience of those who have experienced formal exclusion, and this historic pattern of racial inequality will continue to be experienced unless it is affirmatively acknowledged and altered.

Without the cooperation of those concerned with race and gender justice in building this new progressive agenda, the dialogue will continue to be polarized, divisive, and adversarial. Unless we can build the concerns of racial and gender inclusion into the process of collaboration, these issues will continue to be addressed in settings that undermine the capacity of institutions to adapt to changing conditions.

In addition, research consistently shows that ignoring patterns of racial and gender exclusion causes these patterns to recur. A proven method of minimizing the expression of bias in decision-making consists of reminding decision-makers of the risk of bias or exclusion and requiring them be fair and unbiased. Unless we continue to pay attention to the impact of our decisions on members of groups that are the target of subtle bias and exclusion, those group members will continue to be marginalized.

Fairness

Using the margins to rethink the whole-by using performance   to develop opportunity-will help with fairness as well as   functionality. The functional approach to selection reduces the   importance of criteria that have excluded women and people   of color and favored wealthier applicants. It enables   previously excluded people to "show their stuff." Moreover,   by rethinking the standards of selection for everyone, this   approach destabilizes the idea that the existing meritocracy is   fair. Embedding the role of diversity enables other people to see how benefiting women and people of color benefits them.   In addition, the functional approach has the potential to create   a participatory and accountable selection process, which can   enhance individuals autonomy and institutions legitimacy.

Finally, conditions for sustained contact, genuine collaboration, and fair assessment provide outsiders with a meaningful opportunity to learn, perform, and succeed. Studies of multi-racial teamwork suggest that the opportunity   to work as relative co-equals in interdependent, cooperative   teams may also reduce bias.

 Indeed, carefully structured, accountable, and participatory   work groups may replicate the conditions most likely to   reduce bias and permit genuine participation by women and   people of color.

To be sure, these more interactive and informal forms of selection and management rely explicitly on discretion and subjectivity. Preconceptions and biases will likely affect evaluations of performance in ways that often exclude women and people of color. And unstructured discretion exercised without accountability or participation by diverse decisionmakers will likely reproduce biased and exclusionary results. But these biases have not been eliminated by formal selection practices and paper-and-pencil tests. More importantly, the model of formal fairness that is outcome-driven, rule-bound, and centralized will not reach many of the places where women and people of color seek to enter.

If the economy is moving in the direction of creating and restructuring work along more team-oriented, participatory lines, we need approaches to selection and performance that permit women and people of color to participate fairly and to succeed in this changing environment. Otherwise, women and people of color will remain on the margins of the new economy. Moreover, as business entities become more fluid and rely more on subcontracting and temporary work, we must devise new and more interactive strategies for inclusion and empowerment that embrace a workforce existing in the margins of traditional legal categories. The exercise of discretion cannot and should not be eliminated. Instead, discretionary decision making must become the subject and site of participation, accountability, and creative problemsolving.

A Democratic Imperative

Access to work and education is a fundamental attribute of modern citizenship. Work provides an identity that is valued by others. Work organizes and shapes the citizen's sense of self. Virtually every aspect of citizenship is channeled through participation in the workplace. For most people, medical care, pensions, and social insurance are linked to workplace participation. In these ways, work has become a proxy for citizenship.

Increasingly, the opportunity to work in a non-contingent, fulltime position that provides these benefits of citizenship depends on access to higher education. People who are not educated do not get jobs, and thus cannot participate in the responsibilities and benefits of citizenship. Moreover, those without the benefits of higher education increasingly work in shifting, temporary, and task-centered jobs. Such individuals may fail to develop a sense of personal worth, institutional or communal loyalty, or positive agency, all attributes essential to functioning as citizens.

In addition, voting-the process that has traditionally served to permit participation and influence public decision makingdoes not afford individuals the capacity to deliberate and exercise much influence over the conditions of day-to-day life. Without the opportunity to participate in intermediate institutions, such as places of work and schools, many citizens have no sense that their voices are being heard.

If, as we believe, work and education are basic

components of citizenship, screens or barriers to participation should be drawn in the least exclusive manner consistent with the institution's mission. Access and opportunity to participate is critical to equipping citizens to fulfill their responsibilities, to respecting their status and autonomy as individuals, and to legitimating society's decisions as reflecting the participation of the community. People who feel they have a voice in the decision-making process are more likely to accept the ultimate decision as legitimate, even if it is different from the one they initially supported.

Through the first two centuries of our nation's history, restrictions on voting based on race, gender, and wealth were gradually lifted "only after wide public debate" about "the very nature of the type of society in which Americans wished to live." These barriers were invalidated because they came to be seen as unduly burdening access to this fundamental aspect of citizenship. Courts also recognized that these burdens, through the exercise of selective discretion by local officials, fell disproportionately on dis-empowered groups such as African Americans.

We believe a national debate on the terms of participation in equivalent forms of citizenship is long overdue. Just as "history has seen a continuing expansion of the scope of the right of suffrage in this country,"

So we would argue that 21st-century democracy will depend on a commensurate expansion of the scope of access to higher education and opportunities for on-the-job training. Even if there are justifications for requirements relating to the capacity to exercise citizenship responsibilities effectively, these requirements must be drawn in the most narrow way possible because of the importance of assuring democratic access and legitimacy in the distribution of citizenship opportunities and responsibilities.

A performance-based framework of selection is the equivalent, in employment and education, to the elimination of poll taxes and restrictive registration laws in the arena of voting.

We seek to open up a conversation about issues that many people treat as resolved. Our institutions do not currently function as fair and functional meritocracies. Only by rethinking our assumptions about the current system and future possibilities can we move toward the ideals that so many Americans share. This enterprise offers the possibility of bringing together many who are adversaries in the current affirmative action debate but share an interest in forging fairer, more inclusive, and more democratic institutions. It reconnects affirmative action to the innovative ideal. In this way, affirmative action can reclaim the historic relationship between racial justice and the revitalization of institutions to the benefit of everyone.

CRIME

Violence Against Women Act Reauthorization: Summary and Highlights

On October 28, President Clinton signed into law the Violence Against Women Act (VAWA) of 2000. This bill was the culmination of years of hard work by many members of Congress and advocates from across the country to reauthorize and expand the programs created under the original VAWA, passed in 1994. VAWA II, passed as part of the Victims of Trafficking and Violence Protection Act (H.R.3244), dedicated resources and focused energy on many new issues, while funding proven programs at favorable levels.

Dating Violence:

One highlight of the new law was the inclusion of dating violence in several VAWA programs. STOP grants, Grants to Encourage Arrests, Rural Domestic Violence and Child Abuse Enforcement Grants, and Grants to Combat Violent Crimes Against Women on Campus are now expanded to address dating violence. While all VAWA grants and programs were not amended to include dating violence, its inclusion in parts   of the bill was a significant victory for advocates, victim   service providers, and victims.   Sexual Assault:

VAWA 2000 strengthened the nation's response to sexual assault victims and increased support for sexual violence programs and coalitions. The new law directed the attorney general to evaluate existing standards of training and practice   for performance of sexual assault forensic exams and to   recommend a national protocol. The law almost doubled the   previous funding authorization for Rape Prevention and   Education Grants, while setting aside 2.5% of STOP grant   funds each fiscal year for sexual assault coalitions (2.5% is set   aside for domestic violence coalitions as well). In addition,   25% of civil legal assistance grant money authorized under   VAWA 2000 must be used for projects that focus on providing   legal assistance to sexual assault survivors.

Courts:

VAWA 2000 aimed to engage the courts in the effort against   domestic violence, sexual assault, and stalking by making the   courts eligible to receive funds (STOP grants and Grants to   Encourage Arrests) for training court personnel. In addition,   grants for education and training for state and federal court   judges and personnel were reauthorized for five years.   Furthermore, training on child abuse for judicial personnel   and practitioners is funded at $2.3 million each year for fiscal   years 2001 through 2005.
Improvements and New Provisions:
Several other significant measures passed as part of the

final language: restored and strengthened protections for battered immigrant women; improvements to Full Faith and Credit provisions; pilot programs for transitional housing and supervised visitation centers; and programs addressing violence against older or disabled individuals. Rural Grants, Court Appointed Special Advocate funding, Community Initiatives to Prevent Domestic Violence grants, support for the National Domestic Violence Hotline, and funding for battered women's shelters were all reauthorized at satisfactory levels in VAWA 2000. Finally, the law extended the federal stalking statute to include stalking via the Internet. The following chart summarizes VAWA 2000's major new provisions, various amendments to original VAWA programs, and authorization levels through 2005. An expanded chart

Elder Fraud

Elder Victims of Crime

I believe as a nation, we have not faced this issue squarely-for two primary reasons.

First - the elderly in this country are ignored. We live in a fastpaced, youth-oriented society. Elder issues are not high on the   social agenda. Many of our parents and grandparents live their   twilight years in isolation and loneliness.

Second - policy debates about crime and its victims focus on   victims of violent crime, virtually to the exclusion of victims   of nonviolent property crimes. It is the firm belief of our   organization that every crime has a victim and every victim   needs this nation's help. Nonviolent crime can be emotionally,   physically, and spiritually devastating. And, because they have   particular difficulty being their own advocates, elderly victims   have a special claim on our social conscience.

So, you are to be commended for drawing national attention to   the plight of elderly victims of fraud. After working with nearly 10,000 public and private non-profit agencies and organizations across the country, it is clear   to us that elderly victims of fraud are among the most   underserved of any victim group. You just heard three people   describe their experience, but every day there are thousands of   cases like theirs: people scammed by home services, defrauded   by caregivers, exploited by neighbors or family members, or   tricked by the unscrupulous.

Best estimates are that 20% of the elderly have been victims   of some kind of fraud.

Unfortunately, many elder victims are too embarrassed to report. Sometimes the perpetrator is a loved one or their caregiver, and they don't want to get them in trouble. Sometimes, elders are not aware they have been defrauded or   feel that reporting will do no good, or they don't want to   bother the police. Sometimes, they are reluctant to confront   their greatest fear - that they will be considered incompetent to   handle their own financial affairs. By reporting, many feel they   risk their independence.

Even when elder victims of fraud do report, it is often to Adult   Protective Services, or another agency already providing   services to them, and it is common for their complaints not to   be passed on to the police.

Finally, for cases that find their way to the criminal justice system, police, prosecutors, judges, and jurors may discount   elderly witnesses, failing to distinguish between mental   incapacity and physical infirmity.

As other witnesses have testified, the impact of fraud on elders   can be profound and life altering. Elders, more often than not,   live on fixed incomes, many at or below the poverty level. Too   often, fraud means elderly Americans go without food,   medication or other necessities.

As elders lose their savings, go into debt, mortgage property,   or take out credit card advances to pay those exploiting them,   even comfortable lifestyles collapse.

Generally, senior citizens do not have the time or opportunity for financial recovery; their prime earning years are behind

them. At a time in life when one tries to conserve assets, a blow to financial security is often a permanent and lifethreatening setback.

Elder fraud victims often find their trust shattered. They doubt their judgment. They feel isolated, depressed, angry, and ashamed. These violations of trust compounded with the subsequent uncertainty about paying bills, often lead to illness. In fact, seventy-eight percent of elderly victims develop acute and chronic anxiety.

Even when elders do reach out, help is rarely available. As a nation, we don't address the needs of victims of nonviolent crime. Every state in this country has a financial compensation system that pays for medical and counseling expenses, and other costs of a crime. None cover elder fraud.

Furthermore, a recent national survey of victim assistance programs reveals, only 8 of the 184 responding programs indicated that they intervene on behalf of elder abuse victims, including victims of financial exploitation.

Between 2010 and 2030, it is estimated that the proportion of Americans over 65 will grow to 20% of our nation's population. We must do better, we must do more, and we must act soon.

Older Americans served this country well. They deserve dignity and financial security, and yet they are too frequently   robbed of both. We urge you to lead a national discussion on   this problem and help construct effective responses. Our   elders deserve no less. We pledge our continued support to   you in these efforts.

Gun

Polic

y

the regulation of guns as consumer products   personalized guns childproof guns   mandatory registration of handguns   mandatory safety training for all gun owners restricting gun purchases by criminals   restricting concealed-carry licenses   the regulation of private gun sales

Every Gun Owner should be required to Register their firearm   and be issued a Gun Owner's Registration ID Card by the   Department of Justice.

Every Gun and   long Gun   should have a Ballistic Fingerprint   record with the Department of Justice..

MEDICARE
THE
LIFEBOAT

. EXECUTIVE SUMMARY

Since Medicare was enacted in 1965, it has provided
health   care security to millions of America's seniors and
people with   disabilities. Medicare is the binding
commitment of a caring   society to our most vulnerable
citizens, and a commitment   that America must always
keep.

As successful as the Medicare program has been, it has not
always kept pace with decades of dramatic improvements
in   health care. As a result, Medicare beneficiaries today
lack   many of the choices and benefits available to
millions of other   Americans. Medicare still does not
provide an outpatient   prescription drug benefit, forcing
many seniors to go without   the medicines they need.
Medicare does not provide full   coverage for important

preventive health care, such as cancer or diabetes screenings, and it does not offer protection against uncapped medical costs that can rob seniors of their savings. Moreover, with health care costs on the rise and the Baby Boom generation nearing retirement, Medicare faces serious financial challenges. This will require Medicare to make the best use of today's modern health care delivery methods to maximize the benefits for current and future participants while addressing the long-term sustainability of the program. President Bush believes our nation has a moral obligation to fulfill Medicare's promise of health care security for America's seniors and people with disabilities. To meet this obligation, the nation must act now to bring Medicare into the 21st Century by providing more choices and better benefits to every senior in America.

In July 2001, the President outlined the following principles for Medicare reform:
5. All seniors should have the option of a subsidized prescription drug benefit as part of modernized Medicare.
6. Modernized Medicare should provide better coverage for preventive care and serious illness.
7. Beneficiaries should have the option of keeping the traditional plan with no changes.
8. Medicare should provide better health insurance options, like those available to all federal employees.
9. Medicare legislation should strengthen the program's long-term financial security.
10. The management of the government Medicare plan should be strengthened so that it can provide better care for seniors.

11. Medicare's regulations and administrative procedures   should be updated and streamlined, while the instances of   fraud and abuse should be reduced.
12. Medicare should encourage high-quality health care for   seniors.

The President today is proposing a Framework to Modernize   and Improve Medicare that builds on these principles. He   looks forward to working with Congress on legislation this   year to bring more choices and better benefits to Medicare.   The President has committed up to $400 billion over the next   ten years in his FY 2004 budget to pay for modernizing and   improving Medicare.

The President's framework will give all Medicare beneficiaries   access to:
+   Prescription drug coverage that enables seniors to get   the medicines they need, without the government dictating   their drug choices.
+   Choice of an individual health care plan that best fits   their needs-just like Members of Congress and other federal   employees enjoy today.
+   Choice of the doctor, hospital, or place they want for the   treatment and care they need.
+   Full coverage for disease prevention such as screenings   for cancer, diabetes and osteoporosis.
+   Protection from high out-of-pocket costs that threaten to   rob seniors of their savings.
The President will make sure that low-income seniors receive   additional financial assistance so they will not have to pay   more to receive better benefits than they currently do under   Medicare.

For too long, political pressures have kept our nation from bringing the benefits of modern health care to Medicare. The President is calling upon members of both political parties to work together with him to pass legislation this year. More Choices - Including the Choice to Stay in Traditional Medicare

The President believes Medicare beneficiaries should be given more choices in how they receive their heath care-and these choices should be strictly voluntary.

Those seniors who are happy with their current coverage in traditional Medicare will be able to keep that coverage and receive help with the high costs of prescription drugs. Traditional Medicare will continue to be there for those who want it with help for prescription drugs. But seniors who want more choices and better benefits-including a prescription drug benefit, full coverage of preventive care and limits on high out-of-pocket costs-will be able to select options providing these additional benefits as well. Seniors will have the right to select the health plan that fits their needs best-rather than a one-size-fits-all government plan.

Better Benefits-Including Prescription Drug Coverage

Option 1-Traditional Medicare
Those who are satisfied with the current Medicare system will   continue receiving their care as they do today with help for the   high costs of prescription drugs. These beneficiaries will gain   access to discounted drugs through a prescription drug   discount card-estimated to achieve savings of 10-25% on the   cost of prescription drugs-as well as coverage to protect them   against high out-of-pocket prescription drug expenses.

These new benefits will be provided at no additional premium.

Option 2-Enhanced Medicare

Enhanced Medicare will give seniors the same types of choices   that are available to members of Congress and other federal   employees. In every area of the country, Medicare beneficiaries   will have multiple health plans from which to choose. These   plans will offer prescription drug benefits, full coverage of   preventive benefits, protection against high out-of-pocket drug   costs, and cost sharing that does not penalize participants who   need the most medical care. Again, the decision to choose Enhanced Medicare will be entirely up to each senior, and participants will be able to choose any doctor or any hospital   they want for the treatment and care they need.

The President's framework will ensure that the benefits offered under Enhanced Medicare are sufficiently attractive to   seniors, relative to traditional Medicare, to guarantee that   Enhanced Medicare is a viable system.

Option 3-Medicare Advantage

Seniors will also have the option of enrolling in low-cost and high-coverage managed care plans, similar to those available today under Medicare. Medicare Advantage will include plans that offer a subsidized drug benefit, and all plans will be able to offer extra benefits, as many private plans do today. Immediate Discounts for all Seniors

To ensure that seniors are provided help as soon as possible, the President will ask Congress to immediately provide all seniors with a drug discount card that is estimated to achieve savings of 10 to 25 percent on the cost of prescription drugs by pooling the buying power of Medicare participants.

Additional Help for Low-Income Seniors

Under the President's framework, low-income Medicare beneficiaries will get prescription drug coverage without paying additional premiums and will receive additional assistance with their cost-sharing. The President will ask Congress to provide low-income seniors immediately with a prescription drug discount card, as well as a $600 annual subsidy for drug coverage, which will continue for lowincome seniors who stay in traditional Medicare. This subsidy can be added to their discount card at the point of sale, or alternatively paid to existing Medicare Choice health plans that enroll low-income seniors and provide them with prescription drug coverage.

II. A FRAMEWORK TO MODERNIZE AND

IMPROVE MEDICARE

Background

Since Medicare was enacted in 1965, it has provided health care security to millions of America's seniors and people with disabilities. The program was established using the most current insurance models of its day and has proven successful in extending coverage to some of society's most vulnerable members. Today, Medicare provides health care coverage for 40 million Americans. Enrollment is expected to reach 77 million by 2031, when the Baby Boom generation is fully enrolled.

As successful as Medicare has been, it has not kept pace with decades of dramatic improvements in health care delivery. As a result, Medicare today does not provide the benefits and choices that are available to many other Americans. The program lacks an outpatient prescription drug benefit, full coverage of many preventive benefits, and protection from high out-of-pocket costs.

Medicare's current hospital coverage illustrates the need to update the program. Instead of providing more coverage for patients when they get sick and go into the hospital, Medicare actually requires them to pay more when they need to stay longer in a hospital. This is just the opposite of what Americans in most private health plans experience today.

Many participants in Medicare bolster their Medicare coverage with supplemental policies (Medigap) or retiree health   insurance. Some seniors-those with the lowest incomes-are   eligible for coverage from Medicaid. But many seniors do not   have access to affordable supplemental assistance, leaving   them vulnerable to the high costs of serious illness.

Twenty-four percent of Medicare participants lack any drug coverage, millions more have very limited drug coverage, and many cannot afford the drugs they need to maintain their health and prevent serious illness (see below).

Absent substantial reform of the Medicare program, the situation is certain to worsen. Premiums for Medigap plans, particularly those with drug coverage, have increased considerably over the past three years and are often unaffordable for participants of modest means. At the same time, employers find it increasingly difficult to fund retiree health care, and many have reduced or eliminated these benefits.
To ensure that Medicare provides a secure health care future for today's seniors and future retirees, the nation must act now to modernize and improve the program. The President has committed up to $400 billion over the next ten years to pay for modernizing Medicare, and looks forward to working with Congress to develop and pass legislation this year.

President Bush's framework will give all Medicare beneficiaries access to:
+   Prescription drug coverage that enables seniors to get the medicines they need, without the government dictating their drug choices.
+   Choice of an individual health care plan that best fits their needs-just like Members of Congress and other federal employees enjoy.
+   Choice of the doctor, hospital, or place they want for the treatment and care they need.

+   Full coverage for disease prevention such as
screenings   for cancer, diabetes and osteoporosis.
+   Protection from high out-of-pocket costs that threaten to
rob seniors of their savings.

More Choices-Including the Choice to Stay in Traditional Medicare   A key part of modernizing and improving Medicare is adding   flexibility to the program so that Medicare participants have   the right to more choices in how they receive their careincluding the choice of staying exactly where they are today.

Those who have coverage they value in traditional Medicare   will be able to keep that coverage and receive help paying for   the high cost of prescription drugs. Traditional Medicare will   continue to be there for those who want it with help for   prescription drug costs.

But seniors who want to have more choices and better benefits-including a comprehensive prescription drug benefit,   full coverage of preventive care and limits on high out-ofpocket costs-will have that choice as well.

They will be able to enjoy the same types of choices that   members of Congress and other federal employees do.

If Congress passes legislation this year, then these choices will   be available beginning January 1, 2006. In the meantime, to   give seniors more immediate help with prescription drugs, the   President is proposing to make a prescription drug discount   card available to all seniors and to provide an additional $600   subsidy to low-income participants for their prescription drug   costs.

Better Benefits-Including Prescription Drug Coverage

Option 1-Traditional Medicare

Seniors currently enrolled in traditional Medicare could continue receiving their care as they do today through the current benefit structure with additional help for the high cost of prescription drugs. Part B premiums for participants in traditional Medicare would not be affected by the creation of Enhanced Medicare.

Additionally, beneficiaries remaining in traditional Medicare will be able to receive coverage to protect them against high out-of-pocket prescription drug expenses, at no additional premium. They can also choose to receive a drug discount card like all seniors.

Participants who are satisfied with their current coverage could also continue receiving coverage from supplemental sources, including former employers, Medigap or Medicaid. The President's framework will add two new Medigap plans to the existing ten standardized plans. These new plans will include prescription drug assistance, additional protection against high out-of-pocket costs, and would reduce, but not eliminate, deductibles and co-payments.

Option 2-Enhanced Medicare

Under Enhanced Medicare, seniors will receive a choice of plans similar to those offered to federal employees and members of Congress through the Federal Employees Health Benefit Plan (FEHBP). The choice of plans would be available to all seniors regardless of where they live. Enhanced Medicare will offer benefits described below and standard drug coverage (or an equivalent benefit package). As with traditional Medicare, the federal government will pay for most of the cost of coverage under Enhanced Medicare, with participants paying a smaller share. Beneficiaries who enroll in an average priced plan in their region would pay a premium for the medical portion of their coverage equal to the Part B premium.

Under Enhanced Medicare, seniors will be able to choose any doctor, any hospital, in any place for the treatment and care they need. Additionally, Enhanced Medicare plans will offer seniors the option of further limiting their out-of-pocket costs through supplemental coverage.

Enhanced Medicare will include the following benefits:
+ Prescription Drug Coverage: Under Enhanced Medicare, plans will offer a subsidized prescription drug benefit with a monthly premium, an annual deductible, coverage of prescription drug costs and protections for those who have high drug costs. Low-income seniors will receive this drug coverage for no additional premium and will receive additional subsidies to limit their copayments.

To provide an array of choices in benefit design and to encourage plan innovation, plans will be free to structure their offerings differently, provided the benefit meets a basic federal standard. Further, plans will be required to show that any changes they make to the standard benefit package are not meant to attract only healthy enrollees or discourage the sick or people with disabilities from joining.

+ Full Coverage of Preventive Benefits: Currently, Medicare covers certain preventive services only after the Part B deductible is met. In addition, many preventive services require co-insurance. Enhanced Medicare plans will provide full coverage of preventive services. Full coverage will remove the financial barriers for low-income seniors, who are less likely to seek preventive treatment, such as prostate cancer screenings and mammographies.

+   Protection from High Out-of-Pocket Costs: Traditional   Medicare does not protect patients from uncapped costs.   Enhanced Medicare will eliminate the lifetime limit for   inpatient hospital care and protect against high medical bills   for hospitalizations. In Enhanced Medicare, participants with   very high out-of-pocket costs will face no additional cost   sharing. Traditional Medicare does not limit these costs.

+   Fairer Cost Sharing: Currently, traditional Medicare penalizes its sickest participants by requiring them to pay more   when they need to stay longer in a hospital. At the same time,   Medicare requires cost-sharing for some services, but not for   others. For example, patients pay 20 percent or more when   they visit their doctor or a hospital outpatient department, but   those needing home health care pay nothing out-of-pocket.

Under Enhanced Medicare, participants will have a single deductible for medical services, like that in most private insurance plans, to provide better protection from high expenses for all types of health care. The single deductible will   replace the separate Part A and Part B deductibles. Additionally, after a lower deductible, participants would pay   nothing for their first two inpatient hospital admissions in a   year and a reasonable copay for any subsequent admission.   These changes will provide better protection for participants   who need the most medical care. Further, Enhanced Medicare   will have sensible cost-sharing requirements on all other   services, including limits on out-of-network cost sharing.

Assistance for Low-Income Seniors in Enhanced Medicare

Under Enhanced Medicare, low-income participants who are not eligible for Medicaid will receive financial assistance with out-of-pocket prescription drug costs. Lowest income participants will pay no drug premiums or deductibles and will pay only nominal cost sharing, regardless of their level of outof-pocket spending. States would determine eligibility for low-income assistance.

Administration of Enhanced Medicare

Enhanced Medicare will be administered by a new Medicare Center for Beneficiary Choices (MCBC) under the Department of Health and Human Services.

The MCBC will designate large, multi-state Medicare regions. In each region, seniors and people with disabilities will have several Enhanced Medicare options. The chart below illustrates one way in which these large, multi-state regions might be structured.

Plans will submit bids to the MCBC for the opportunity to serve one or more of the Medicare regions, and plans will have to accept any Medicare participant wishing to enroll regardless of whether the beneficiary lives in a rural or remote area. This approach minimizes risk selection and guarantees access for all seniors to these plans, as is the case with the Federal Employees Health Benefit Program.

Option 3-Medicare Advantage

In addition to Enhanced Medicare, seniors will have the

option   of enrolling in the same type of low-cost and high-coverage   managed care plans that are available today under Medicare.   Currently 5 million Medicare participants choose to get their   benefits and receive additional services from such plans. These   plans often offer broader coverage at a lower cost than the combination of Medicare and Medigap plans that many seniors

choose.

Under the newly created Medicare Advantage program, plans   in competitive markets will bid to provide participants with   Medicare's enhanced basic benefit package. Participants who   select more efficient plans will benefit from savings, and some   participants in the most efficient plans could pay no premium   at all and potentially qualify for a rebate on their premium.

Advantage plans will continue to be a good choice for participants willing to accept a more selective provider panel   in exchange for lower cost sharing and extra benefits. Creating   a system in which different types of delivery systems compete   for participants' business will result in a marketplace where   plans in each system will have strong incentives to provide the   most efficient and highest quality care. Efficient plans will be   able to offer extra benefits and/or reduced cost sharing.

Advantage Plans will also be able to offer a benefits package   without drugs for those participants who are satisfied with   drug coverage they already have. Just as in Enhanced   Medicare, low-income seniors will pay no additional cost for   a drug benefit offered through

Medicare

Advantage plans. Other enrollees will pay a monthly premium to pay for their share of the prescription drug benefit costs.   Immediate Discounts for all Seniors

A Medicare-endorsed prescription drug discount card will provide an opportunity for all seniors to get discounted drugs as Medicare transitions to a modernized system. All participants, for a nominal enrollment fee (waived for lowincome seniors), will be able to join a discount card plan. The card will let them pool their buying power with that of other participants to obtain manufacturers' discounts, with savings from 10 to 25 percent. No longer will uninsured seniors face the highest retail prices of any group. In addition, drug card sponsors, which could include Pharmacy Benefit Managers and other entities, will publish comparative information on drug prices to help seniors make smart buying choices.

Additional Help for Low-income seniors

Under the President's framework, low-income seniors who enroll in Enhanced Medicare will get prescription drug coverage without paying additional premiums and will receive   additional assistance with their cost-sharing for prescription   drugs. Like all seniors, they will be eligible to receive   immediately a Medicare drug discount card, at no cost, which   would provide them with estimated savings of 10 to 25   percent on the price of prescription drugs. In addition, lowincome seniors will receive an added subsidy of $600 annually   to pay for prescription drugs. The subsidy will be added to   their discount card and work like other federal electronic   benefit transfer programs, with the card providing the subsidy   at the point of sale. The subsidy could alternatively be paid to existing Medicare+Choice plans that enroll low-income seniors and provide them with prescription drug coverage.

SUMMARY

The President's framework for Medicare will provide more choices and better benefits for all seniors. If legislation is passed in 2003, then beginning next year, seniors will have the following benefits:

In 2004:

All seniors will receive access to discounted drugs (discount of 10-25%) through Medicare-endorsed prescription drug discount cards.
All low-income seniors will have access to drug discounts through the card, and an additional $600 per year to assist in purchasing prescription drugs.

In 2006:
Seniors will have the option of staying in Traditional Medicare and receiving a prescription drug discount card, coupled with coverage that would protect them against high out-of-pocket costs for their prescription medicines.
All seniors will have access to at least three new Enhanced Medicare plans that offer:
o   comprehensive prescription drug coverage;
o   full coverage of preventive care; and
o   protection against high out-of-pocket medical costs.
Seniors will still have the option of choosing a Medicare Advantage plan that will offer prescription drug coverage and other benefits in a managed care setting.
Conclusion: Medicare for Today and Tomorrow

President Bush is committed to ensuring that Medicare will   always be there for seniors and people with disabilities. His   ideas for modernizing and improving Medicare build on the   strengths and successes of the current system, while   guaranteeing that all seniors will have access to a prescription   drug benefit and other benefits Medicare does not offer today.   Under the President's framework for Medicare, seniors will   have the right to the same type of health care benefits enjoyed   by members of Congress and other employees of the federal government. Low-income seniors will not pay more for additional benefits.

To improve, Medicare must have the benefit of modern health   care delivery systems and methods that have proven successful   in the private sector. The President's initiative will introduce   private sector innovation and competition to the Medicare   system to help keep costs reasonable, ensure high quality care   and begin to address Medicare's long-term financial   challenges.

While Medicare must be modernized and improved to meet   the needs of its current participants, the program must also be   made sustainable for future generations. Given the financial   challenges Medicare faces in the future, changes to the   Medicare program we make today must not exceed our   nation's means to deliver them tomorrow.

Seniors have waited too long for a modernized Medicare with a prescription drug benefit. It is time for members of both political parties to work together to pass legislation this year that will modernize and improve Medicare for seniors today and tomorrow.

OUR

NATIONAL

PARKS

Prepared by the staff of the NRPA Division of Public Policy,   Washington, DC Legislative Issues and Analysis - 108th   Congress   By   NRPA Staff <mailto:nrpapolicy@aol.com> National Recreation and Park Association   Legislative Issues   and Analysis - 108th Congress Overview-108th Congress

As the 108th Congress begins, The NRPA Division of Public   Policy provides this update to key supporters and advocates on   the current status of congressional organization, legislator   assignments, and legislation to authorize and appropriate   funds that are a priority for parks and recreation.

Early indications are that the Republican majority in both houses of Congress, led by a Republican administration, will advance a strongly ideological and conservative agenda for the 108th Congress.

Republican majority in the House indicates that most legislative proposals will have smoother sailing in the House than in the razor thin Republican majority of the Senate, but there is clearly a sea change in the balance of power in Washington.

A strongly conservative agenda is not necessarily an anti-parks and recreation agenda. In fact, except for some notable exceptions such as the Urban Park and Recreation Recovery Act (UPARR) and the Physical Education for Progress Program (PEP), park and recreation related legislation may fare as well as any other discretionary spending during what is bound to be a contentious Congress. Plans to implement certain regulatory changes relating to public lands bear close watching. Impacts are not known at this time.

A growing budget deficit, a bad economy, and an impending war in the Middle East have severely impacted virtually all discretionary spending. After much contention, the FY 03 budget was just passed by the Senate, at an amount that is consistent with the President's priorities. The House will take up the FY 03 budget during the week of January 27, 2003, and there will be pressure to pass the current year budget sooner rather than later.

FY 2004 budget proposals from the Administration are expected to be significantly lower in several program areas of importance to NRPA. The potential impacts on

NRPA priority programs are uncertain at this time, but there is deep concern for some key programs.

The President's State of the Union address is scheduled for January 28 and his budget will be transmitted to Congress on February 2.

An Overview of NRPA Priorities
NRPA's primary interests in this legislative session are grouped in three areas:

+   Appropriations - Land and Water Conservation Fund (LWCF) State Assistance; Urban Park and Recreation Recovery Act (UPARR); Incentive Grants for Local Delinquency Prevention Programs (Title V); Delinquency Prevention Block Grant Program; Juvenile Accountability Block Grant Program; Physical Education for Progress (PEP); 21st Century Schools; Special Recreation Program; Workforce Investment Act Youth Programs: Federal Lands to Parks; Rivers, Trails, and Conservation. NRPA will support the work of others where recreation and park or similar values will result. These include appropriations for USDA Resource Conservation and Development Districts, for example.

+   Reauthorizations/Amendments - Transportation Equity Act (TEA 21); Child Nutrition Programs; Rehabilitation Act; Individuals with Disabilities in Education Act; and Urban Park and Recreation Recover Program.

+ New Legislation - Urban and Rural Disease Prevention and Health Promotion Act, the Improved Nutrition and Physical Activity Act (IMPACT); the Highlands Stewardship Act; and other selected park, recreation, and public lands related bills.
Federal Funding Interests for Parks and Recreation (Selected Programs Only)

DEPARTMENT OF AGRICULTURE

Child Nutrition Program Reauthorization
The Child Nutrition Act first authorized the Summer Food Service Program (SFSP) and the Child and Adult Care Food Program (CACFP) in 1966. SFSP is an entitlement program designed to provide funds for eligible sponsoring organizations, including public park and recreation agencies, to serve nutritious meals to low-income children when school is not in session. CACFP provides federal funds for meals and snacks served at after-school programs for school-age children, including park and recreation sponsored after-school programs, and to adult day care centers serving chronically impaired adults or people over age 60.

When school is out, low-income children lose their access to regular daily school lunches and breakfasts. The Summer Food Service Program and summer National School Lunch Program participation combined still reach barely one in five (21.2) of the low-income children eligible for free and reduced price meals during the regular school year. Park and recreation agencies can help to increase the number of lowincome children who eat healthy meals during the summer. Participation levels are much higher than in the late 1980s and early 1990s but since the 1996 welfare law cut reimbursement amounts for food and ended Summer Food Service Program start-up grants, program expansion has essentially stopped. There is a need to reinstate appropriate reimbursement amounts for meals and snacks. Lowering eligibility requirements for low-income youth from 50 percent to 40 percent of all youth would also help more agencies to be able to sponsor the SFSP and CACFP programs. In addition, park and recreation agencies could also use start-up funds to initiate the programs.

In the latter part of 2000, Congress created a pilot project to reduce paperwork and increase reimbursement in the states with low participation rates in the SFSP. This pilot program should be expanded nationwide so that more public park and recreation agencies operating these programs can benefit from reduced administrative requirements.

DEPARTMENT OF EDUCATION

21st Century Community Learning Centers Program   The focus of this program, re-authorized under Title IV, Part B, of the No Child Left Behind Act, is to provide expanded   academic enrichment opportunities for children attending low   performing schools. Tutorial services and academic   enrichment activities are designed to help students meet local   and state academic standards in subjects such as reading and   math. In addition 21st CCLC programs aid youth development   activities, drug and violence prevention services, technology   education programs, art, music and recreation programs,   counseling and character education to enhance the academic component of the program. The FY 2003 Labor HHS Education bill faces a $2.7 billion cut, to $131.4 billion from   the Senate bill approved by the Appropriations Committee last   summer.

The FY 2002 appropriation was $1.0 billion.   NRPA will recommend at least $1.1 billion.

Special Recreation Demonstration Program (sec. 316) This program provides ôseedô or expansion funds for the development of recreation and related services for individuals   with disabilities to aid their employment, mobility,   independence, socialization, and community integration. Over   the past 19 years, many public park and recreation agencies   have used funds from this program to initiate therapeutic   and/or inclusive services for individuals with disabilities.   Once these programs are in place, the communities generally   continue investment in them; 75 percent of the Special   Recreation programs continue after federal funding is   discontinued.

And these services often make a huge difference in the lives of the people they serve-assisting their independent functioning,
ability to find work, and self-esteem.
For fiscal year 2002, the Administration requested no funds for this program, which usually receives $2.6 million. NRPA Public Policy, working with the Alliance for Disability, Recreation, and Sport, has advocated for reinstatement of these funds.

NRPA will continue to work to ensure at least $2.6 million is appropriated for this important program. Individuals with Disabilities in Education Act Reauthorization

The Individuals with Disabilities in Education Act is the landmark legislation that requires public schools to provide free and appropriate education services to students with disabilities. Each student is required to have an Individualized Education Program (IEP) that describes his/her annual educational goals and the services that s/he will receive throughout the school year. Related services, including recreation and therapeutic recreation, are included among the services for students with disabilities eligible for reimbursement under this law.

When recreation is provided as a related service, it can help students develop functional, recreation, and academic skills necessary for development in the cognitive, physical, behavioral, social, and affective domains. For instance, cognitively, recreation can help reinforce academic, and decision-making skills, and problems-solving abilities.

In addition, therapeutic recreation can be a helpful transition   service for students with disabilities, connecting them with   community contacts and job-related skills that can help them   transition into adulthood.

NRPA will work to ensure that recreation services are defined   appropriately and that the individualized education plan   include annual measurable goals related to and functioning in   the learning environment and community integration. IDEA   should also acknowledge the positive behavioral supports that   TR offers and its usefulness as a transition service.

Rehabilitation Act Reauthorization

The Rehabilitation Act was first authorized in 1973 and last   amended in 1998. The law authorizes the Department of   Education to provide grants to states for supportive   employment programs and it funds federal programs of the   Rehabilitation Services Administration (Department of   Education), including the Special Recreation Demonstration   Program (sec. 316) for individuals with disabilities.

The North Carolina Division of Public Health recently conducted a study that suggests that individuals with disabilities suffer from chronic health conditions significantly   more than individuals without disabilities. Active recreation   can help prevent the development of secondary disabilities.

Therapeutic recreation can also help individuals with disabilities improve self-confidence and job-related skills for individuals with disabilities. Currently, the employment rate of individuals with disabilities is only about 40 percent, about one-half of the rate for individuals without disabilities. Meanwhile, the Special Recreation program is in danger of elimination by the current Administration. A new program that would provide grants for inclusive and therapeutic recreation programs for individuals with disabilities with an emphasis on employment and physical activity outcomes is necessary. A new program that would provide grants for inclusive and therapeutic recreation programs for individuals with disabilities with an emphasis on employment and physical activity outcomes is necessary. This grant program should be authorized at a minimum of $20 million.

DEPARTMENT OF THE INTERIOR

Land and Water Conservation Fund State Assistance
LWCF grant resources are available to state and local
governments for the conservation of land and water
resources   and recreation development and access. All
state and local   grants require at least a 50 percent match
by the non-federal   partner. Since 1965, LWCF has
assisted over 38,000 nonfederal projects. State and local
governments assume all   operation and maintenance
activities. Program revenues   annually are appropriated
from a U.S. Treasury account with a   balance in excess of
$10 billion. The act directs that $900   million from OCS
revenues be deposited annually. FY 2002   funding was
$144 million. House passed FY 2003 funds   totaled $154
million. The FY 2003 informal agreement for a   budget of
$18.95 billion would cut $850 million from the   House
passed $19.8 billion budget proposal. The Senate is
presently considering a revised fiscal year 2003
appropriation   of $115 million. If adopted, this amount
will be reconciled   with the House.
NPRA recommends $200 million for FY 2004
LWCF   state/local assistance.

Urban Park and Recreation Recovery

The UPARR program provides direct federal matching
assistance to cities and urban counties for rehabilitation of
existing recreation and park facilities. It encourages
systematic   local planning and commitment to continuing
operation and   maintenance of recreation programs, sites,
and facilities. Three   types of grants are available:
Rehabilitation grants (70%   Federal and 30% Local),

154

Innovation grants (70% Federal and 30% Local) and Planning grants (50% Federal and 50% Local). The FY 2002 appropriation of $30 million supported over 70 local projects. FY 2003 proposed funds ($30 million House, $10 million Senate), are at high risk under the HouseÆs self-imposed spending limits.

NRPA will recommend $50 million for FY 2004. DEPARTMENT OF JUSTICE The FY 2003 Commerce, Justice, and State bill faces a $2.1 billion cut, to $41.3 billion from last years Senate Bill. Incentive Grants for Local Delinquency Prevention Programs (Title V)

The Office of Juvenile Justice and Delinquency Prevention (OJJDP) provides grants for programs to address the problems of delinquency prevention within communities that experience high crime rates. Each state receives block grants to distribute to local delinquency prevention programs; public recreation agencies are eligible to apply. NRPA will encourage appropriations of sufficient funds to address program needs and will discourage earmarking of funds.

NRPA appropriation request to be determined.

Delinquency Prevention Block Grant Program (newly authorized)

The Juvenile Justice and Delinquency Prevention Act reauthorization of 2002 authorizes the OJJDP administrator to make grants to states who can then provide subgrants to governmental agencies and non-profit organizations for projects designed to prevent juvenile delinquency. Local units of government may apply jointly for this program with at least two private non-profit agencies that experience in working with youth. Examples of eligible activities include: developing locally coordinated policies and comprehensive programs among education, juvenile justice, recreation, non-profit, and social service agencies; projects to reduce juvenile participation in gangs that commit crimes; and after school programs that target at-risk youth and youth offenders.

NRPA appropriation request to be determined.

Juvenile Accountability Block Grant Program
Since 1998, Congress has appropriated the Juvenile Accountability Block Grant Program funds that have been used primarily for developing incarceration facilities and juvenile courts. This program received an annual appropriation of approximately $250 million. But until now, none of these funds could be used for prevention or community services. In the new law, the grants can be used for the development, implementation, and administration of graduated sanctions to juvenile offenders that include restitution and community service. Other eligible activities include establishing and maintaining accountability-based restorative justice programs, programs to reduce recidivism among juveniles, and programs to enhance school safety. Local units of government are recipients of sub-grants from grants provided to states. This program is authorized at

$350   million for fiscal years 2002 through 2005. NRPA appropriation request to be determined.

DEPARTMENT OF LABOR

Youth Opportunity Grants/WIA Youth Formula Programs
The Administration has targeted Youth Opportunity grants
for elimination, suggesting that youth would be better
served by the Job Corps program. But the Youth
Opportunity program targets youth who live in extremely
impoverished communities and it does not have the same
eligibility requirements as the Youth Formula programs,
so more youth in need can access these services. The
Administration has also proposed cuts in the Youth
Formula programs, which generally receive over $1
billion from the Department of Labor. These grant
programs are viable funding sources for park and
recreation agencies operating youth programs, especially
those agencies involved in the NRPA National Youth
Congress program.
NRPA will recommend $250 million for Youth
Opportunity Grants and at least $1.1 billion for Youth
Formula Funding in 2004.

DEPARTMENT OF TRANSPORTATION

Transportation Equity Act/Recreational Trails Program
The long-awaited re-authorization of Transportation
Equity Act would fund various highway and trail
development and maintenance programs at fixed annual
amounts for 6 years. Currently the RTP program, also
authorized by TEA-21, provides funds to develop and
maintain recreational trails for motorized and
non-motorized recreational trail users. Each state
determines application dates and selects Recreational
Trails projects differently. TEA-21 is due for
reauthorization in FY 2004.

The program currently provides $50 million annually in

recreation trails funding and advocates are proposing an increase on the premise that federal tax revenues for recreation and tourism fuel consumption are not reflected accurately in the currently authorized funding level. Most recreation trails coalition members will request $150 million annually for the reauthorization of the recreation trails program, a $100 million increase.

The Transportation Enhancements (TE) program, a component of TEA-21, supports restoration of historic transportation facilities, bicycle and pedestrian facilities, landscape enhancements and beautification. Eligible activities for grant funds include safety and educational activities, environmental mitigation, and habitat connectivity projects. Over $600 million is available for transportation enhancements under current law.
The Congestion Mitigation Air Quality program provides funds for cities and counties to improve air quality, including the development of non-motorized transportation such as trails and paths.

In addition, NRPA will work to modify language for the Jobs Access Reverse Commute (JARC) program, which links lowincome persons to job support services. NRPA would like to see eligible activities such as transportation to child care, after school programs, and therapeutic recreation services specifically referenced in TEA-3.

NRPA supports the inclusion of New Freedom demonstration and community grants that would help ensure transportation for persons with disabilities. TEA-3 should also include funds to collect and analyze data that assesses the relationship between disease prevalence and the number and quality of trails, bike paths and other active recreation supports in communities. NRPA supports reauthorization of the Act and sufficient additional funds to address these identified needs.

ANTICIPATED LEGISLATION, 108TH CONGRESS
Urban and Rural Disease Prevention and Health Promotion Act

The Urban and Rural Disease Prevention and Health Promotion Act of 2002 (H.R. 5306 in the 107th Congress) will be introduced by Rep. Bernie Sanders (I-VT). It would provide grants and loans to public agencies for the development of indoor disease prevention and health promotion centers in urban and rural areas throughout the United States. For fiscal year 2003, it would authorize $100 million.

Recent studies proclaim that almost two-thirds of adults in America are overweight or obese and approximately 15 percent of children and adolescents are overweight or obese. Clearly there is a need for interventions, on the municipal level, to encourage people of all ages in America to be more active. Smaller jurisdictions are often limited in their ability to develop recreation facilities.

A federal grant program that sets aside half of the grants for   municipalities with populations under 50,000 would allow many more small cities and towns to develop such facilities   for their residents. Public park and recreation agencies would   likely manage the development of these facilities.   Improved Nutrition and Physical Activity Act (IMPACT)   Senator Bill Frist (R-TN), and others, are expected to reintroduce the Improved Nutrition and Physical Activity Act   (S.2821 and H.R. 5412 in the 107th Congress) in 2003. Title   II of IMPACT would create a local grants program, for which $40 million would be authorized in fiscal year 2003. Cities,   counties, tribes, and states could use these grants to: plan for   or promote bike paths and other physical activity   infrastructures; form partnerships to develop wellness   programs, nutrition programs, and other programs to increase physical activity, especially among older and younger populations; and to promote the use of recreational facilities   during after school hours and weekends. This bill would   provide funds for health program operations-it could fund, for   example, activities related to the Hearts Parks program or   other wellness programs.

The Bear & Wilderness Protection Act is a measured I sponsored. The Shoot a Bear Go to Jail measure will protect California Wildlife.

CALIFORNIA BEAR & WILDERNESS PROTECTION ACT of 2006

INITIATIVE MEASURE TO BE
SUBMITTED DIRECTLY TO THE VOTERS

The Attorney General of California has prepared the following title and summary of the chief purpose and points of the proposed measure: (Here set forth the title and summary prepared by the Attorney General. This title and summary must also be printed across the top of each page of the petition whereon signatures are to appear.)

TO THE HONORABLE SECRETARY OF STATE OF CALIFORNIA We, the undersigned, registered, qualified voters of California, residents of_____ County (or City and County), hereby propose amendments to the Fish and Game Code and to the Revenue and Taxation Code, relating to the protection of bears and wilderness and petition the Secretary of State to submit the same to the voters of California for their adoption or rejection at the next succeeding general election or at any special statewide election held prior to that general election or otherwise provided by law.

The proposed amendments (full title and text of the measure)

read as follows:

Section 1. This act shall be known and may be cited as
the   Bear and Wilderness Protection Act of 2002.

Sec. 2. Chapter 12 (commencing with Section 2950) is
added   to Division 3 of the Fish and Game Code, to read:

Chapter 12. BEAR AND WILDERNESS PROTECTION

2950. The Bear and Wilderness Protection Trust
Fund is   hereby created in the State Treasury for the
purpose of   administering and implementing this
chapter.

2951. Notwithstanding Section 13340 of the
Government   Code, all money deposited in the Bear
and Wilderness   Protection Trust Fund in each fiscal
year is continuously   appropriated, without regard to
fiscal year, as follows:

(a) One-half to the department to acquire, restore, and
enhance   wilderness habitat, including the creation of bear
safe zones,   coastal marine safe zones, game refuges, and
wilderness   restricted use districts, as provided in this
chapter.

(b) One-half to the Department of Parks and Recreation to

restore, repair, and enhance the existing state park system, as provided in this chapter.

2952. (a) The department shall purchase and acquire real property to create bear safe zones, coastal marine safe zones, game refuges, and wilderness restricted use districts, as described in this section, for the purpose of protecting bears and other wildlife.

(2952) The department shall designate certain wilderness areas as "bear safe zones," to be used as bear sanctuaries. The department shall capture, transport, and release all bears and wildlife that may wonder into urban communities and return bears and wildlife into the bear safe zones. The public may enter a bear safe zone with a permit issued by the Department of Fish & Game, but it is unlawful to possess a firearm or Bow or Archery based killing device in a bear safe zone.

(2953) The department shall designate certain coastal areas as "coastal marine safe zones," to be managed by the department for the protection of fish and marine life. No fish or marine life may be taken from a coastal marine safe zone without a permit issued by the department for that taking.

(2954) The department shall designate certain wilderness areas as "game refuges," to be managed by the department for the preservation and protection of wildlife species, as identified by the department. The public may enter game refuges, but no game animal or other animal may be taken without a permit issued by the department for that taking.

(4) The department shall designate certain areas as "wilderness   restricted use districts," to be managed by the department for   the preservation and protection of all wildlife and wildlife   habitat. No public access may occur in a wilderness restricted   use district without a permit issued by the department for that   access.

(b) The department shall consider the following factors in establishing bear safe zones, coastal marine safe zones, game   refuges, and wilderness restricted use districts:

(4) The bear safe zones, game refuges, and wilderness restricted use districts shall be established in rural areas so as   to minimize conflicts between wildlife and human activity.

(5) Sites shall be established in areas where an abundance of   wildlife is already in existence. The department shall maximize   its resources to provide for the largest possible sites.

2953. The department shall organize and sponsor wilderness   outreach programs directed at inner city youth and offer   wilderness educational programs for children in kindergarten   and grades 1 to 12, inclusive.

2954. The department may use funds appropriated pursuant to   subdivision (a) of Section 2951 to hire additional staff to   carry out its duties under this chapter, including, but not   limited to, hiring additional management and support staff,   fish and game wardens, criminal investigators, and other enforcement officers. The department may also use those funds to purchase vehicles and other equipment necessary to carry out its duties and enforce this chapter.

2958. The Department of Parks and Recreation shall restore and repair the existing state parks system, and shall purchase and acquire additional land, rivers, wetlands, historic sites, and other resources, in order to enhance the state parks system.

2959. The Department of Parks and Recreation may use funds appropriated pursuant to subdivision (b) of section 2951 to hire additional staff to carry out its duties under this chapter, including, but not limited to, hiring additional management and support staff, park rangers, park safety officers, environment officers, and other enforcement officers. The Department of Parks and Recreation may also use those funds to purchase vehicles and other equipment necessary to carry out its duties and enforce this chapter.

SEC. 3. Chapter 9 (commencing with Section 4750) of Part 3 of Division 4 of the Fish and Game Code is repealed.

SEC. 4. Chapter 9 (commencing with Section 4750) is added to Part 3 of Division 4 of the Fish and Game Code, to read:

CHAPTER 9. BEARS
4750. (a) It is unlawful to take, injure, possess, transport, import, or sell any bear or any part or product thereof, or to conspire to take, injure, possess, transport, import, or sell

any   bear or any part or product thereof.

(b) A violation of this section is a felony
punishable as   follows:

(1) A person 18 years or older who is convicted of
violating   this section for noncommercial purposes shall
be subject to a   fine of ten thousand dollars ($10,000) and
sentenced to five   years imprisonment in the state prison,
without opportunity

for parole or credit for good behavior.

(2) A person 18 years or older who is convicted of
violating   this section for commercial purposes shall be
subject to a fine   of fifteen thousand dollars ($15,000) and
be sentenced to 15   years imprisonment in the state prison,
without opportunity   for parole or credits for good
behavior.

(3) A person under the age of 18 who is convicted of
violating   this section for commercial or noncommercial
purposes shall   be placed under the care of the
Department of the Youth   Authority for five years.

(c) The Office of the Attorney General is responsible for
prosecuting any person who violates this section. The
Attorney   General may authorize County District Attorney
and City   Attorney Offices to further enforce this measure.
The Attorney   General will provide training to Law
Enforcement agencies to   support this measure.

(d) Notwithstanding any other provision of law, a
person   arrested for violating this section for

commercial purposes may not be released on bail unless the court determines that the person does not pose a flight risk.

SEC. 5. Section 12005 of the Fish and Game Code is repealed.

SEC. 6. Section 6051.5 is added to the Revenue and Taxation Code, to read:

5. (a) In addition to the taxes imposed by Section 6051, 6051.2, 6051.3, and any other provision of this part, for the privilege of selling tangible personal property at retail, a tax is hereby imposed upon all retailers at the rate of one-half of 1 percent of the gross receipts of any retailer from the sale of all tangible personal property sold at retail in this state on and after 30 days of passage of this measure.

(b) All revenues received pursuant to this section shall be deposited in the State Treasury to the credit of the Bear and Wilderness Protection Trust Fund created pursuant to Section 2950 of the Fish and Game Code.

SEC. 7. Section 6201.5 is added to the Revenue and Taxation Code, to read:

6201.5 (a) In addition to the taxes imposed by Section 6201, 6201.2, 6201.3, and any other provision of this part, an excise tax is hereby imposed on the storage, use, or other consumption in this state of tangible personal property purchased from any retailer on and after 30 days of passage of this measure, at the rate of one-half of 1 percent of the sales price of the property.

(b) All revenues received pursuant to this section shall be deposited in the State Treasury to the credit of the Bear and   Wilderness Protection Trust Fund created pursuant to Section   2950 of the Fish and Game Code.

SEC. 8. This act shall become operative on 30 Days of   passage by the Voters of the State of California.

SEC. 9. If any provision of this act or the application thereof   to any person or circumstances is held invalid, that invalidity   shall not affect other provisions or applications of the act that   can be given effect without the invalid provision or   application, and to this end the provisions of this act are   severable.

SEX CRIMES
A Wildfire!

Like other violent crimes, the incidence of rape has fallen every year since 1992, according the Federal Bureau of Investigation's annual crime report and the Justice Department's National Crime Victimization Survey. But the first National Violence Against Women survey says more than twice as many rapes are committed each year as official statistics indicate.

The new survey, commissioned by the U.S. Centers for Disease Control and Prevention (CDCP) and the National Institute of Justice, based its estimates on detailed interviews with 8,000 men and 8,000 women.

+   The CDCP survey estimated more than 876,000 rapes are committed in a typical year in the U.S., compared to the 432,000 rapes estimated to occur by the National Crime Victimization Survey.

+   Unlike FBI figures for rape, it includes males who have been raped by men or women -- which it estimates occurs about 111,000 times a year -- and children younger than age 12.

+	Also, the CDCP survey estimates one in seven American women have been raped, lending support to advocates of rape victims and others who argue rape is holding steady or growing while other violent crime declines.

+	The survey says the typical female rape victim is raped nearly three times a year, often by her husband or domestic partner.

However, criminologists say rapes have declined. The official FBI crime report, based on rapes actually reported to police, shows a 12 percent decline since 1993. And the National Crime Victimization Survey -- which is considered more accurate because it includes crimes not reported to the police
   shows a 60 percent downturn in rape between 1993 and 1996.

Experts also point to the shrinking pool of men ages 29 or younger, the group that accounts for more than half of all rapes, as support for the reported decline. And they say a nationwide move to longer prison sentences for violent offenders is keeping convicted rapists off the street longer. 1 Rape Case is too much! The California Child Protection Act is an option to consider

EVANS
CHILD
PROTECTION
ACT

A BALLOT MEASURE for 2006

: *Mervin L. Evans*

Imposes surtax on alcoholic beverages of 25 cents per container or per serving. Directs surtax to be deposited into a trust fund administered by the Attorney General for financial support for sex crimes victims, for law enforcement training, and for grants for local law enforcement, prosecutors, and child social services. Increases penalties for specified sex crimes to 50 years without parole where the victim is a minor and to 25 years without parole where the victim is a woman. Requires individualized determination of bail for such crimes. Summary of estimate by Legislative Analyst and Director of Finance of fiscal impact on state and local governments: Measure would result in increased special fund revenues from the new alcoholic beverage tax ranging from $1 billion to $2 billion annually, and comparatively modest other state and local revenue effects; increased state General Fund prison costs, eventually reaching $800 million annually in 2048-49 for state operations and totaling $1.9 billion for capital outlay; and increased tax administration costs potentially ranging up   to several million dollars annually.

www.ingramcontent.com/pod-product-compliance
Lightning Source LLC
Chambersburg PA
CBHW080249290526
45790CB00005B/1752